Deception

An Essential Guide to Understanding How Machiavellian People Can Hide the Truth and Use their Knowledge of Human Behavior to Manipulate, Negotiate, and Persuade

Contents

Introduction

You are most likely reading this because you're curious about "dark psychology." But what does it even mean? Is it some form of dark magic possessed only by a few people well versed in the art of controlling others? Or is it more like a Harry Potter thing with the soul-sucking, happiness-draining dementors? In this book, you will finally get your questions about dark psychology answered with clarity.

Dark psychology is the science and art of using mind control and manipulation to get what you want. Where psychology is about learning about human behavior and how people generally interact with one another, dark psychology focuses more on coercion, persuasion, motivation, and manipulation tactics.

Already, you might wonder whether or not you would want to "manipulate" anyone, and whether you should even be reading this book. If this is you, it would be wise to go ahead and read this. The world is not all flowers and roses, and you'd be doing yourself a huge favor learning about the dark triad, especially Machiavellians, who this book is primarily about. Having this awareness will prepare you for any eventual meeting with one of these people.

Some people read books like this because they would like to learn how to manipulate everyone around them. If this is you, here is a note: Be sure that you use everything you learn here for the greater good.

Machiavellianism is one of three manifestations of dark psychology or the dark triad. The thing about the dark triad is that, often, possessing these traits is a great predictor of troublesome relationships and a blatant disregard for law and order. The narcissist is the one who displays grandiosity and egotism unparalleled, along with a distinct lack of empathy. The psychopath is a charmer, your friendliest friend, and often impulsive and selfish, with no capacity for remorse or empathy. Finally, there is the Machiavellian who is a master of deception and has no qualms exploiting people if it means they get what they want, unfettered by such frivolous things as "morality," which regular folks hold dear.

Unlike other books on this subject, this one is up to date and easy to understand. If you are a beginner—just learning about dark psychology—you will find this a friendly guide on Machiavellian ways. If you're well versed in these matters, you will very likely learn new things. This book is written in a straightforward, easy-going style, so you won't struggle with the concepts.

Throughout the pages, you will come to understand the true nature of a Machiavellian. You will learn how they are so skilled at deception and how they use what they know about you to persuade and control you.

What you're about to learn is extremely potent and should be used only for good purposes. What you do with this knowledge, in the end, is entirely up to you.

Chapter One: Introduction to Dark Psychology

There are people you run into every day for who persuasion and manipulation is an elevated art form. These people are often experts at wearing masks from the moment they step out into the world because if the world were to see what truly lies beneath their masks . . . well, it probably wouldn't bode very well for them.

The Dark Psychology Triad

Here is what makes up this triad:
- Narcissism
- Psychopathy
- Machiavellianism

The narcissist is the most self-centered person you will ever meet, has no empathy, and believes that everything about them is larger than life itself. Dare to challenge this thought process, and they will make you regret it.

The psychopath is ever charming. This would not be a problem if they weren't also completely lacking in empathy—like the narcissist. They are very impulsive and have no remorse. You probably know the saying, "Some people just want to watch the world burn?" Well, "some people" are basically psychopaths.

Now the Machiavellian. No one lies better than this member of the dark triad. They do not just lie for the heck of it, either; they'll tell whatever tales they must if it means getting people to do their bidding. They have no morals, and for them, people are simply toys to be manipulated as they see fit. The Machiavellian sees nothing wrong with lying if it means they get their way. Don't bother trying to preach them a sermon; a Machiavellian understands how humans think and feel and uses this knowledge to their advantage. However, you most likely will be unaware of their complete grasp of human nature. This is part of what makes them so effective in their tactics . . . and dangerous.

Manipulation: More Common than You Realize

You may think that these people exist on the fringes. Odds are, you won't run into someone so manipulative. However, this manipulation goes on every day. Sure, you may not be the specific target of a Machiavellian, but more people than you realize have to deal with their lies.

In fact, you will find that manipulation happens all around you. You'll find it in sales letters, commercials, Internet ads, radio ads, television, newspapers—the works. As a parent or guardian, you will have to deal with this sort of behavior from teenagers as they discover who they really are and try to figure out the best way to get what they want and express their autonomy.

Don't be alarmed, but more often than not, dark manipulation and persuasion techniques are used by the people nearest and dearest to you, the ones you love and trust.

Everyday Manipulative and Persuasive Tactics

In case you still want to hold on to the notion that you are not a witness to manipulation and persuasion each day, perhaps a simple list of such tactics will help you see the truth.

1. *Giving the silent treatment.* You may have experienced or witnessed this for yourself, where someone deliberately gives you the cold shoulder, won't speak to you, and even goes to great lengths to avoid running into you.

2. *Love bombing.* Giving compliments and showing love and affection only to get someone to soften up enough to ask them for a favor.

3. *Denying love.* Ever heard of a spouse or lover withholding affection from their significant other to get them to apologize or do something they wouldn't otherwise?

4. *Lying.* Telling flat-out or "white" lies and embellishing stories here and there to seem more interesting.

5. *Boxed-in choices.* The manipulator gives you only a couple of options, which serve to keep you from realizing that there are other options you can choose besides the ones they've presented.

6. *Manipulating semantics.* Here, the manipulator uses words that can easily mean a million different things. When you confront them later on, they tell you they meant something entirely different from what you thought.

7. *Reverse psychology.* The manipulator asks you to do something, knowing fully well you'd rather do the opposite of what they ask, and expecting you to follow through on your own "original" thought.

Perhaps you are starting to realize how common manipulation is, or you may realize you have even used a few of these tactics yourself. The point is to let you know it is not too hard to fall prey to these techniques, no matter who or where you are. It happens at work, in friendships, families, relationships, media, politics, religion . . . everywhere.

Now, this is not to say that everyone who uses any of these tactics is necessarily a part of the dark triad. Sometimes, people are unaware of what they're doing and how wrong and unethical these methods are. Children are very impressionable, so many people learn these tactics just from observing adults or strong influences in their lives. Some people learned these manipulation techniques in the process of living their teenage lives. Some people learn these tricks later in life and usually coincidentally, not out of a need to control others. They used a technique and got their desire handed to them on a silver platter, so they continue with these methods to make it further along in life.

Additionally, some get actual training in the art of manipulation and persuasion. You can use programs to learn how to get your way most of the time, using tricks that are often very unethical. This is especially the case when it comes to making sales or being involved in the marketing world. With these dark tactics, they can drum up desire and literally flip a switch in your mind that tells you you have absolutely got to have the product du jour. You think you got a good deal when really, they're the ones who rake in most of the money and benefits.

Meet Possible Members of the Dark Triad

Just what kind of people are a part of this group?

Politicians. Though there are some good ones, many often use dark manipulation tactics to get people to see things their way. They do and say what they must to get people on their side. Some convince themselves it's for the greater good; others are conscious of being in it only for themselves.

Attorneys. Some attorneys will stop at nothing to win a case. They'll use dark tactics to sway things their way, and they won't feel a shred of remorse over being unethical.

Leaders. Several leaders have mastered the art of dark persuasion. They use the most devious methods to make sure their followers fall in line and continue to bend over backward to deliver better and better performance.

Salespeople. If you've ever read a sales letter, you probably think you're merely reading a bunch of words advertising a particular product, and there is nothing more going on. However, a lot is going on when you consider the subtext of these sales letters' messages. They're deliberately written to trigger primal emotions in you that make you act just the way the writer wants you to.

Public speakers. Public speaking is another arena where you'll see dark persuasion thriving. The public speakers use these techniques to get their audience hooked and make sure that they keep coming back for more and spending more money on the next tier product and the next event.

Generally, selfish people will also use these techniques because what better way to make sure they always get what they want? As far as they are concerned, everyone else can burn.

It may seem as though this book is glorifying the process of using dark methods to manipulate everyone and get your way, and it may seem like that is really the best way to go. However, in the end, going dark is never worth it. When people and businesses get into these techniques, over time, there is a lack of trust. You can only fool people for so long before they wise up to your game.

A Matter of Ethics

So how can you tell when you are ethical as you attempt to persuade or motivate someone? It is really as simple as assessing your intentions. You must be honest in your assessment. You have to figure out why you're trying to persuade or motivate someone to take action. Are you trying to help them? There is nothing wrong with helping yourself in the process, as long as whatever your end game is, it's mutually beneficial for all parties involved.

A good rule of thumb is to make sure that you aim to create a win-win situation no matter what you are doing. You must not goad yourself into assuming something is really good for the other party just to assuage your conscience. It needs to be a true win.

What Drives the Darkness?

There are many reasons why people with dark triad personalities do what they do. Sometimes, it is a matter of being accepted. For others, it's about getting ahead in life, becoming more successful in work, or getting paid a lot of money. Others still are simply in it for the glory of power and the feeling of being in control of everything and everyone. Some are driven by their love for religion or political leanings. There is a fair number who are the way they are on account of a psychiatric disorder.

The thing to understand about these dark predators is that they can be anyone—from any country, race, religion, or economic standing. So, do not be quick to dismiss your seemingly kind and charismatic preacher or leader or philanthropist simply because you expect they want the best for everyone, more than most.

No One is Blameless

The truth is: Everyone can express dark triad traits. They have the ability to take it so far, past the point of no return, where they only ever see everyone around them as prey and hunt for no reason other than because they can.

You should know what this is referring to. Sometimes you have that one, wicked, dark thought that comes out of nowhere, sometimes forcing you to ask, "Where did that come from?" This should not worry you, though, because most people never act out those thoughts. For the narcissists, psychopaths, and Machiavellians, not only do they express those dark inclinations, but they also draw a lot of pleasure and satisfaction from doing the thought(s). They also think that the people who fall prey to their antics deserve it since they were too naive and got swept up in their manipulations. They actually become addicted to their predatory behavior.

Today, with the advent of the Internet and the world shrinking into a global village on account of social media, it is very important to become aware of these dark inclinations that certain members of the human race harbor. When you also factor in the anonymity that the Internet grants every cybercitizen, you can surely see how, more than ever, people with dark personalities can thrive and go beyond the limits they otherwise had before social media and the Internet existed.

The rest of this guide focuses on "the Machiavellian" and how they wield deception ever so skillfully against regular folk to achieve their devious desires. Having established that monsters are masquerading as regular people, now turn your attention to the matter of deception. What counts as deception? Who do people consider deceptive, and under what situations is that deception malevolent, if at all?

Chapter Two: What is Deception?

Deception is the act of misleading people. It is about keeping the truth hidden, or propagating ideologies and beliefs that are the furthest thing from the truth, usually to get some advantage or advancement. There are many ways that deception can play out, including outright propaganda, distraction—typically in conjunction with sleight of hand—concealment, dissimulation, or camouflage. Deception also includes self-deception. It's all about presenting false claims as truth.

Deception inevitably will be discovered. Upon discovery, it's inevitable that the deceived party feels betrayed and would think twice about trusting the deceiver ever again. When people relate with one another, there is a natural expectation that there will be honesty and transparency. For this reason, deception is the desecration of the rules of a relationship, which are held sacred and dear to humans.

For the most part, if you think about it, you expect that lovers, family, friends, coworkers, and even strangers will be honest. The only time you really expect dishonesty is if you have had to deal with a traumatic experience that leaves you with your guard up, or if you have witnessed or heard of a person's propensity for dishonesty. With that being said, there's still a fair bit of deception that happens, even between you and the one who keeps the other side of your bed warm every night.

Kinds of Deception

Deception comes in various forms, from distortions and omissions of truth to making dishonest claims designed to get the other person to take whatever action you want them to—often at their own expense. Deception can also play out not just in words but in actions as well. Say you want to buy a pair of shoes. You inspect one shoe out of the pair, when some other shopper stands by you, picks up the other, and inspects it. In the process, they may make a face that communicates disgust or dislike, puts the shoe down, and walks away.

Having done that, if you are not someone who is particularly certain of your style, or if you weren't sure about that shoe initially, you will probably begin to see everything wrong with the shoe on account of the way they reacted. So, you just might decide the shoes are not worth the money, put it down, and walk away. Seconds later, the person swings by and decides they actually do like the shoes and buy them. This is a very basic example of how deception can play out in action.

Here are some misleading claims. For instance, a company that manufactures fruit juice may write on the can, "Made with 100 percent real fruit," knowing fully well that most people will see that and decide, "Wow, that's gotta be healthy. I'm buying it." In truth, it could be that the "100 percent real fruit" actually makes up only about three percent of the can. After all, the label says, "made with," not "made of." A more discerning buyer will turn to see the ingredients, which will no doubt begin with "Water, sugar . . ." and find that really what they have is a can full of sugar, preservatives, coloring, and flavoring, with just a pinch of "100 percent real fruit." Sure, the company claim what they made is the truth; however, technically, the fact is that it will lead the buyers to draw false conclusions.

To cut to the meat of the matter, here are the various forms of deception people deal with every day:

1. *Lies.* You're given information that is completely different from the truth.

2. *Concealments.* You're deliberately only given a bit of the picture. The deceiver will leave out critical bits of information that will put what they're saying in the proper context, or they will act in ways that will muddy the relevant facts.

3. *Equivocations.* You are fed very contradictory statements or vague, indirect statements instead of an actual answer.

4. *Understatements.* The deceiver deliberately downplays the most significant parts of the truth to trick you, minimizing their importance.

5. *Exaggerations.* The deceiver will tell you the "truth"—only it's an incredibly stretched version and overstates or magnifies bits that will keep you in the dark.

6. *Misinterpretations.* The deceiver will give you the truth but deliberately misinterpret it.

It is important to note the motive behind the deception. In their paper "Interpersonal Deception Theory," Buller and Burgoon (1996, 202 - 242) identify the following motivations for acting deceptively.

- Instrumental motives: The deceiver lies to keep their resources safe or avoid being punished.
- Relational motives: The deceiver lies to keep their relationships strong or establish new, beneficial ones.
- Identity motives: The deceiver is motivated by the need to protect their image or save face.

You might be tempted to say from your lofty, mighty steed, "Well, I never deceive anyone. I keep everything honest and above board." Well, do you really? Think about the time someone apologized for nail clippings, and you replied, "Oh, it's okay, no big deal," knowing fully well that each *clip* sound brought you a step closer to blowing your lid. Or the time when a friend was feeling down in the dumps about something, and so, desperate to have your good buddy back to their old, cheerful self, you gave a compliment you did not mean, or told them something wasn't their fault—even though you both knew it was. The point is that all sorts of people engage in deception. The trouble is a matter of degree.

In fact, you can almost make a case that deception is something that happens, even in nature. Now take a look at the defense mechanism of camouflage, for instance. The sole purpose of the chameleon is to change its color to match the environment around it. The purpose of the wallaby's coloring is to match its surroundings and make sure they are safely hidden from prey. Even the military uses camouflage uniforms and gear, for this same purpose of appearing inconspicuous, as nothing more than part of the furniture.

Deception also happens in the form of disguise. To disguise something is to make it appear to be someone else or something else entirely. Celebrities, when they need to do everyday things and do not want the paparazzi trailing them everywhere, will often wear disguises or go incognito. A disguise can go beyond just looks. Sometimes, there is a change in natural speech patterns, voice, walking pace, and so on. An example of a disguise is Sherlock Holmes, who would often try to appear as someone else so no one would recognize him.

The disguise can also play out in abstract ways, where it is ideas that are disguised as something other than what they really are. This typically happens in government and the political space as a whole. In other words, this disguise is propaganda. You may have heard the phrase "Peacekeeping mission" and wondered why anyone got shot if the real goal was to keep the peace. Or you may hear the phrase "protective custody" being bandied about when really what is going on is government-sanctioned kidnapping.

What other way can deception occur? Dazzle. Dazzling has the effect of leaving the other party too confused to see the truth or take in the more significant stuff. Take a debate between two high schoolers from different schools. One presents logical facts; the other simply "make their points" by asking rhetorical questions after rhetorical questions, barely giving the audience and the judges any time to think critically and realize that they weren't making actual points. Naturally, the dazzling debate team wins, even though they shouldn't have. Another example of this dazzling deception is when an octopus shoots out a cloud of black ink, so predators do not see it when it escapes.

Who Uses Deception?

People who are defiant by nature. With these people, they are more obvious about their deception. They're often very rebellious and will do all they can to get away with a lot of bad stuff without any consequences. Think of your teen who thinks they're smarter than you and tries to escape the repercussions of their actions. The truth is that there is no point in doing things and getting away with it if they don't have any form of acknowledgment for the feat. For this reason, it is easy to spot them being deceptive.

People with deceptive personality traits. They are not the same as those with full disorders. Typically, this kind of person is passive-aggressive. Often, they do not realize that they're seen as deceptive people. For instance, if you have this sort of person as part of a project, and they really don't want to be involved in it, they might procrastinate or conveniently forget to do important things. When you do confront this individual, they are quick to appeal to your emotions, rather than meet you on a logical level about why they're acting how they are, and how you might both arrive at a solution.

People with a personality disorder. Whether it is someone with a narcissistic personality disorder, obsessive-compulsive disorder, or someone who's paranoid, borderline, or histrionic, the fact remains that there's an inaccurate perception of reality in their minds. They will often try to make you a part of their delusional world.

These people are often motivated by a deep fear of rejection, abandonment, or failure, as well as insecurities. They may have experienced some traumatic event in their childhood that has contributed to them turning out the way they have. For these people, they do their best to keep all this fear and insecurity hidden from everyone, and that is why they will craft their own version of events and rope you into believing it all.

People who fall under the dark triad. These sociopaths and psychopaths are very well advanced in their deception tactics and adept at reading everyone through subtext, body language, and simple observation. Being able to read people with ease, they know what to say or do and how to say or do it so that their prey feels a false sense of security with them.

With the people in this group, there is no form of empathy, kindness, or shred of goodness in them. They are completely comfortable with even taking advantage of those that are nearest and dearest to them. As far as they are concerned, the end justifies the means. If they perceive that the only way to get what they want is to get rid of you, they will do so without hesitation and won't look back. They're experts at wielding abuse in subtle, insidious ways, and often, the victim is hardly ever aware of what is going on until it's too late.

The Truth About Deception

Deception is a prevalent part of people's lives, and it plays a useful part, like it or not. However, not all lies are motivated by personal gain at the expense of another. Most lies people tell are for others' sake, just to make sure that everyone can relate without a hitch. That being said, no one likes to feel like they have just been had.

So, if everyone lies, what is the difference between a Machiavellian and an ordinary Jane or Joe? Motive. Studies also show that deception might be a good thing. In a Philosophize This! Podcast on Machiavellianism, it becomes pretty obvious that Machiavelli was not necessarily postulating that everyone becomes deceptive for the sake of it. The theory is that he only wrote *The Prince* to make it clear that while it is fine to want to uphold moral values like honesty and forthrightness in all aspects of life, it is especially impossible for leaders in politics or in general to be honest if they intend to have any form of stability and peace during their administration.

While casting Machiavelli's intentions in this light does make what he wrote appear less villainous, the fact remains that there are Machiavellians who are not simply trying to rule. They are out for number one, and they will mow down anyone to make it happen.

Chapter Three: Defining Machiavellianism

This chapter begins with the origin of the word "Machiavellianism." Niccolo Machiavelli was a Renaissance writer who wrote *The Prince*. The book is about the various techniques that leaders need to use if they want to have a loyal following and ensure order and stability in the land. It was less about doing what was morally right, and more about doing what needed to be done, no matter the cost.

According to Machiavelli, there are two ways to rule. One way is by the law and supposedly brings peace. The other is by brute force. When the first way does not work out, the leader will have to turn to the second way. As such, the wisest ruler will do well not to make promises with the intent to follow through, especially if those promises are actually not in their best interests.

The Machiavellian view of people is that they are all intrinsically bad, and for this reason, the wise leader would do well to deceive them when they must since the people themselves are not particularly trustworthy. Machiavelli states that people are often easily swayed by whatever it is they need at the moment, so it is easy to use these needs to have them dancing to your tune. In his words, "He who seeks to deceive will always find someone who will allow himself to be deceived."

Machiavelli postulated that the leader must adhere to the laws, ethics, and principles in place when ruling over a state. However, when needed, the leader must also be able and willing to hold on to their power by lying and being cunning. In other words, rather than make like the Red Queen and yell, "Off with their heads," the leader would be wise to use flattery and kindness, even if they do not mean it. It would serve them better to seem gracious, kind, honest, and even religious. Machiavelli says it would be best to have these virtues but be prepared to dump them at a moment's notice when circumstances dictate that would be the best course of action.

Machiavellianism and Psychology

Florence Geis and Richard Christie were the very first researchers to consider Machiavellianism regarding psychology, rather than politics. They described it as a behavior, trait, or attitude. Thanks to these American researchers, Machiavellianism is not a trait that only applies to politicians and leaders, and it doesn't mean the same thing as having an authoritarian personality. It is also not simply a psychopathological matter. Even the most ordinary folk can think like Machiavellians, depending on the situations they are faced with.

Machiavellian Traits

Trait #1: Manipulation. As far as the Machiavellian is concerned, there is nothing wrong with being manipulative. They are at home with deception and trickery. They are ever on the prowl to gain something by being manipulative and deceitful. They're incredibly selfish, insensitive, and downright evil when dealing with others.

Despite how much they absolutely love to manipulate people, Machiavellians always tread carefully. They will only ever strike when they see an opportunity to make trouble, get what they want, and get away with it with no one the wiser.

The Machiavellian always has some justification for the things that they do. They will rationalize their most dastardly deeds to no end and will make you believe that in their shoes, you will more than likely have done the same thing. They have all sorts of weapons in their arsenal when it comes to their deception. They will intrude, flatter you, act like they're very cooperative, and do all they can to maneuver themselves right where they need to be to rip the rug out from under you.

The Machiavellian is not a psychopath, though—as they are on the darkest end of the dark triad. Yes, a Machiavellian is both incredibly insensitive and callous, but the psychopath never has a guilty conscience about what they do. As for Machiavellians, they're not so aggressive. They would rather act with tact.

One thing you should know about the Machiavellian or the Mach is that they have a slew of methods to deceive people. In a study by Geis, Christie, and Nelson (1970, pp. 285 - 313), the subjects had been asked to find hidden objects in a picture, while the researcher noted the amount of time it took to find them all. After they were done, the subjects took on the researcher's role and gave the next set of subjects the same test they'd just finished. When they were through, the researcher asked them to distract and disturb other subjects who were still working on their assignments, to keep them from finishing on time. It was left to the subjects' discretion what methods they used to keep the other people distracted.

This study showed that participants with the highest Mach scores on a Mach test had a diverse and wide range of methods to influence non-Mach subjects. They would lie, withhold information, and ask questions that served to confuse and were completely irrelevant when you looked beneath the surface. They also frequently sighed, hummed, whistled a tune, tapped their pencil repeatedly against the desk, and continued to rearrange all the objects they found on the desk. The Mach's were the ones who came up with the most inventive ways to use such distracting techniques to achieve their goal.

You would be hard-pressed to find a better liar than a Machiavellian. In a study by Azizli et. al, Lies and crimes: Dark Triad, Misconduct, and High-Stakes Deception. Personality and Individual Differences (2016, pp. 34 - 39), carried out to test just how likely the subjects were to lie, the participants were given questionnaires meant to gauge how likely they'd get into deception, particularly the kind with high stakes. In all the scenarios presented in the questionnaires, Machiavellians were clearly at home with deception in all forms. However, they were very eager to be a part of high-stakes deception, even more than the garden-variety psychopath is likely to lie.

All of this being said, the Mach does not feel the need to lie all the time, and they are not always necessarily smooth about it. They do not think it is absolutely a must to tell lies every time their lips start moving. For them, it's simply that lying is necessary to get ahead, especially as the world is full of unreliable people as far as they're concerned—never mind that they probably caused these people to act in unreliable ways, to begin with. For the Machiavellian, when the truth will not give them what they want, the lie is the logical choice.

Trait #2: Amorality. Machiavellians are completely fine with being amoral and disrespecting ethics. For them, it is all about what matters to them, and if there's a moral or ethical rule in between them and what they want, you can bet your bottom dollar they're not going to let that get in their way. They would rather have injustice than fail.

The Mach will continue to test you, provoke you, see where your boundaries lie and how they can break them. The very moment the Mach spots weakness in you, they are going to pounce. If there is money to be made, they're fine with ignoring ethics and are even more eager to do whatever amoral thing is necessary. The fact that the Mach never allows social conventions to control them is what makes them the best manipulators.

Trait #3: Cynicism. You will never find anyone more cynical than a Mach. They believe that you can never trust what anyone says or what they do. They'll often assume that people have the worst intentions, that they're all liars and schemers, and therefore should never be confided in or trusted. For the Machiavellian or Mach, they must ever remain vigilant in case someone decides to take advantage of them. In fact, this often leads to them taking advantage of other people so that they can be the first one to be deceitful. This sort of thinking is how the Machiavellian excuses their behavior. After all, why be kind or honest when the other person is most definitely not.

The Machiavellian sees people as being dishonest even when it comes to themselves, holding an impression of goodness that is really not there. They believe that this false knowledge of self is what makes their victims even more vulnerable.

With this inherent cynicism, a Mach can cause an imbalance in power between you and them. They do not consider you an equal but think of you as inferior and open to manipulation—since they believe they have a firmer grasp on your behavior than you do. In a way, they are right. Many people are driven to do the things they do on account of external factors, rather than because they've decided to take action independently. This is what allows the Mach to step into your life, as an external force, and bend you according to their will to gain something from you.

Trait #4: Coldness. The Mach is reserved and cold. They are indifferent to everything. If you want a lesson in detaching yourself from emotions, the Mach will be the best tutor you could ever have. They do not care how you feel and would rather be rational about everything. They are more about their goals than they are about people, and they pay attention to the things that will benefit them while completely disregarding how you feel about their methods or what they're doing to you.

The Mach can think about all the options in a very cool, detached way. This is advantageous to them because no matter what situation they find themselves in, they know just how to control it. They put their goal front and center, sift through all the information they're getting, and figure out the best options and strategies to allow them to achieve their end. They are not concerned with whether your reaction to their methods is one of approval or disapproval; this person is only concerned with doing what they think is best for them.

You can never distract the Mach with your emotions, no matter how intense or terrible they are. Machiavellianism exists on a spectrum. With a high Mach, you can never get in their way when it comes to gaining a better position, promotion, or making more money. A low Mach cares a lot more about the people in their lives, both at work and at home, and this leaves them in a much more vulnerable position since they do not believe that the end justifies the means.

Trait #5: No empathy. No matter what you are going through, the Mach is both unable and unwilling to consider how you feel or walk in your shoes. They lack empathy. Whether you feel pain or joy, the Mach can't relate to it. They're not the most helpful or selfless people, either, so don't expect them to reach out a hand when you're dangling over the end of a cliff—unless, of course, saving you is a means to an end for them. They don't believe in promoting others and would rather keep you under their thumb than give you a leg up. If you're working with a Mach, you have to do things the way they want it. Don't try to get creative—you'll just be asking for a world of hurt.

The Mach is not big on cooperation, and this is no surprise since they have zero empathy. Even if they've been in your particularly difficult position before and know how inconvenient it is, they just can't be bothered. The last thing they will ever do is allow themselves to cooperate or relate to the pain you feel since this will only keep them from doing what they must. This is what makes the Mach such a skilled, cold-blooded manipulator.

Trait #6: High toxicity. The only thing more toxic than dealing with a Machiavellian is taking a bath in a vat of radium. No matter how much you try to be positive and upbeat, the Machiavellian is like a dark cloud, ever willing and happy to rain on your parade. They are incredibly negative and toxic. Being with them often leaves you feeling drained and beyond overwhelmed.

Trait #7: Narcissism. The Mach is more than likely a narcissist. They have extremely narcissistic traits, like only caring about themselves and having a complete disregard for others' interests. They are anything but generous, thoughtful, or mindful of other people around them. If it is not about the Mach, it has no weight or meaning.

The Mach's Empathy

When it comes to empathy, there are two kinds: cold and hot. Cold empathy is mostly something you know on a logical level. You understand the way other people think. You understand what it is they might feel given certain conditions. You get why they act the way they do, and you understand the evolution of events with each person around you. You use cold empathy to grasp how others would feel or react if you were to take a certain line of action.

You use hot empathy to deal with and resonate with other people on an emotional level. However, the Mach does not care about trying to establish this connection. They have cold empathy but don't bother with hot. The reason they need cold empathy is simple: sometimes, they will need to make you believe they truly care so that they can get what they need from you.

Signs of Machiavellianism

Here is a quick list of signs that you are dealing with a Machiavellian and need to watch your back:

1. They have a laser-like, single-minded focus on *their* interests and ambitions.

2. They are confident in everything they do and say.

3. They are incredibly charming.

4. They are very keen on power and money but display a marked indifference when it comes to relationships.

5. They often resort to flattery.

6. They are at home with deception and lies when they deem it necessary.

7. They are unwilling to think or believe the best about other people.

8. They are not big on values or morals.

9. They are comfortable with manipulating others when they have got to have their way.

10. They are rarely ever empathetic, and when they are, it almost seems manufactured.

11. They never let you know what their real intentions are.

12. They do their best not to get bogged down by emotions or commitments.

13. They do not believe in such things as good or people having a conscience.

14. They are at home with hurting other people to get what they want.

15. When you meet them, they seem really difficult to get to know, and they have an air of aloofness about them.

16. They are not shy about being promiscuous and will often have casual sex.

17. They are experts at reading other people and "reading the room."

18. They are not really warm when interacting with other people socially.

19. They might have serious trouble figuring out how they feel about things.

20. They do not have a grasp on the consequences of what they do and say.

The Machiavellian Scale

As mentioned, Machiavellianism exists on a spectrum. The Machiavellianism scale rates Machs from 0 to 100, using a series of questions in a test. Those who score above 60 are "high Machs," while those who score below 60 are "low Machs."

The low Mach is okay with showing others empathy. They are mostly trusting and honest in their interactions. For them, people are intrinsically good, and success means having good morals. If they are way too low on the Mach scale, that just makes them far too agreeable and submissive.

The high Mach is only all about number one. They are only concerned when something or someone seems to threaten their wellbeing. For them, they must employ deception in their day-to-day interactions. They don't care much for human goodness, because it doesn't exist as far as they're concerned. The Mach will never put themselves in a position where they have to depend on you or anyone else, because they think that is an incredibly foolish and naive thing to do. For them, power matters more than love and relationships. Everything else is meaningless.

Nature or Nurture?

At this point, you might be wondering: Is the Machiavellian born this way, or do they become this way? What is the actual origin of this trait? Would one really be a Machiavellian if they were an ordinary person who decided to read *The Prince* just so they can start acting like an actual Mach?

While Machiavellianism is a trait, it is not the only distinctive feature of a manipulative personality. As previously stated, when a person is truly Machiavellian, they will often score as a high Mach . . . unless they decide to deliberately score as a low Mach to fly under the radar—which is not unusual for these highly deceptive people. The thing is, for the most part, the rest will test as low Machs. This doesn't mean they are incapable of deception—it just means that manipulation and deception are not their baselines.

In the realm of politics, being a Machiavellian means that you are a cynic who will often be very calculating in the ways you acquire power and how you make sure that power never leaves your hands. In psychology, Machiavellianism is a trait that you obtain, where you look at all human interactions through the eyes of a cynic and nothing more. If you are a Mach, you'll know it because everything—as far as you're concerned—is a matter of win or lose.

To be clear, there is most likely some influence from genetics when it comes to whether or not someone is a Machiavellian, or whether they will be selfish, callous, and manipulative. That said, it is not entirely on nature; nurture also plays a part. While the genes may exist, the fact is that your experiences growing up, home life, and the way your parents raised you will most likely contribute to whether you will become a dreaded high Mach. You cannot expect someone who has gone through dozens of foster homes from the day they were born to emerge a regular, normal human being. It is not unheard of, but it's rare.

Science has found that some people are genetically predisposed to being psychopaths. However, even without the genes, if you have had a terrible start to the game of life, you are more likely to be affected, no matter how normal your brain structure is or how basic your genes. This is the same thing, whether it is narcissism, psychopathy, or Machiavellianism.

As for people who deliberately learn what it is like to be a Machiavellian so that they can apply these strategies in their lives, well, it's not hard to see why. This is not an endorsement of Machiavellianism, but it would be untrue to say that there are not specific situations where being a Mach would be advantageous. There are scenarios where even Machs on the lowest end of the spectrum will find themselves having to resort to Machiavellian methods to defend themselves or protect their space.

Say you are homeless and have to move in with a friend, but this friend proves themselves to be anything but a good one over time. They treat you like crap and make it seem to everyone else under that roof like you're a whole world of trouble, attacking you when no one else is watching, or when they won't get caught. You might find yourself backed into a corner where, in order to protect yourself till you move out, you start to act like a Machiavellian. You might deliberately withhold or skew information to get back at them or get more people on your side.

If you are dealing with a toxic work environment, you might find yourself doing anything and everything to get toxic colleagues off your back. You might tell lies to stop people from piling their responsibilities onto you. You might swoop in to claim credit for things that you didn't actually do as a way to warn off the offending colleagues who have made your life difficult. You might even start a few rumors. You do not want to do any of this, and you don't relish it at all, but you realize that to try to stay ethical and above board in such an environment is virtually impossible, as everyone around you would love to play pin the tail on the donkey and there are only so many pins you can take without going bonkers.

Chapter Four: How to Hide the Truth

It is time to talk about lies. Studies have shown that roughly 60 percent of people tell a lie every ten minutes or so. Now, this is not enough to say everyone lies. That being said, you have to agree that 60 percent is not a number you can easily ignore, especially when you put that percentage up against the entire populace in America. A study carried out by psychologist Robert S. Feldman of the University of Massachusetts in 2002, published in the Journal of Basic and Applied Social Psychology, demonstrated that it's hard for most people to have a conversation with others without telling a fib even once.

You might want to exclude yourself from this percentage of "liars," but sometimes you lie without even being aware of it. You tell many white lies—just because they are harmless doesn't mean that you're not a liar. Some lies you tell to make things go better in a relationship or make the other person feel better about themselves, which inevitably makes you more likable. However, it's still all deception in the end.

According to The Day America Told The Truth, a survey on mass morality by James Patterson and Peter Kim published by Prentice Hall in 1991, our parents bore the brunt of our deception with 86 percent of us fooling them often, while we lied to siblings 73 percent of the time, friends 75 percent of the time, and lovers 69 percent of the time. Bear in mind that these percentages mostly pertain to lies about things that aren't really important and won't significantly affect how you relate with the people in your life.

Why People Lie

Who gets to judge a lie as meaningless, and by what criteria? Also, why do people even lie to begin with? The incredible thing about lies is that they are an inevitable part of society. Imagine a life where everyone only ever told the plain truth. Everyone would probably hate each other. Salespeople would sell nothing. Advertising and marketing would not exist. Your parents would wonder why in the heck they gave birth to you. Other people would look at you and your parents—or kids—as a lesson on why you should never have kids. Maybe the whole of humanity would become extinct.

Lying is something people have become so used to that they are now naturals at telling lies and being lied to. It is like a game everyone has agreed to play, and one of the rules is that you do not acknowledge you're playing it.

So, what is it exactly that prompts people to tell anything but the truth, even when under oath? To understand this urge, take a moment to really think about a world where everyone only ever tells the truth. If you cannot imagine it, you should watch the movie The Invention of Lying. Now, this once, be honest with yourself: Would you like to live in that world? Would you be able to handle the brutal truth about you and how people feel about you being flung in your face everywhere you go? Honestly?

Just because you tell lies does not make you a Machiavellian. It all comes down to intent. For the Machiavellian, lying is about having control and manipulating people to get what they want. So, why do ordinary people tell these "white" lies then?

1. *They want to fit in*. Everyone lies about the things they can do or have accomplished so that others think of them as being worthy of

love and admiration. They lie because they want to be picked over the next person when they apply for "that" job or loan. They lie about having seen a movie or read a book they actually haven't because they just want the conversation to keep going without getting sidetracked, or because they're embarrassed to admit they're the one person on the planet who has not yet seen *Game of Thrones*. They tell these kinds of lies just to be accepted as part of a group and feel like they're a part of the whole, so they don't stick out like a sore thumb.

2. *They do not want to be punished.* From as young as two years old, people figured out that they could get away unscathed if they lied about something, with no punishment or consequences. Since then, people have learned to tell cover-up tales or one-liners to cover their hides and make it seem like their lapses in judgment or actions never happened.

3. *They do not want to hurt others.* One of the biggest reasons people lie is because they don't want others to be hurt by the truth. This happens a lot when you care for someone, as in a deep friendship or romantic connection. That said, lying in these situations can sometimes be a terrible idea. Say you are about to end a relationship for a very good reason. Maybe your partner is a slob or inconsiderate. It would be better to let them know so that they can do better in their next relationship, or they'll just remain as they are, never learning or growing. Sometimes, you also need people to be blunt with you. If you're not working as hard as you could, or if you did something wrong but were unaware of why it was wrong, in times like this, honesty really is the best policy.

4. *They want things to work out.* Whether you like it or not, lies have always played a very important role in getting the outcomes you prefer. You'll notice this when applying for work, as most people tend to embellish their résumés. Certain professions necessitate using persuasion tactics to get people to buy some product or service or vote for a particular candidate. Here, this is specifically referring to sales, advertising, marketing, and politics.

At this point, it should be pretty clear that lies are virtually unavoidable in people's day-to-day lives. They tell these harmless white lies to pave the way toward their hopes, goals, dreams, and better relationships with everyone around them.

Pathological Liars

If everyone is guilty of lying, what's the difference between you and a pathological liar? Pathological lying is a different beast altogether and is often a sign that the liar might have a mental health problem, like a personality disorder.

When you lie, you are making a statement that is not true so that you can deceive others to gain something from them, whether it's a better relationship or something material. Non-pathological lying is nothing unusual, and it doesn't mean you're not "all up there" when you lie to your kid about Santa. On the flip side, a pathological liar will tell lies compulsively. There is never any clear benefit or reason for them to lie—they just can't help themselves.

Pathological lies are told with zero motivation. Usually, when you lie, you have a solid reason. You do not want someone to be mad at you, or don't want to miss out on something, or want to help someone else feel better, or, or, or . . . With pathological lying, there is just no definite motivation, and you can't quite fathom why they'd bother to tell such a lie to begin with.

It is not particularly obvious whether or not the pathological liar is aware of their deception, or if they can even reason through their lies and figure out whether or not they are logical. Pathological lying is a very problematic thing, as it makes it really difficult to socialize with the liar, who has more likely than not shoved everyone away from them with all their lies.

Causes of Pathological Lying

Unfortunately, there has not been enough research carried out on this, so whatever causes pathological lying remains unknown. No one can tell if the lying is a condition all on its own, or if it's merely a symptom of an entirely different condition. The fact that telling compulsive lies is part of a few well-known conditions like personality disorders and factitious disorder makes it really difficult to figure out.

Factitious Disorder

Factitious disorder or Munchausen's syndrome is a unique condition where the affected individual will act like they are mentally or physically unwell when, in truth, they're actually fine.

There is also Munchausen's syndrome by proxy. In this condition, the affected individual will often lie about someone else having some disease or illness. For the most part, this syndrome affects mothers who will act like their kids are unwell and tell lies to their doctor about their child's condition.

It is unclear what causes this disorder, but here are a few theories: Childhood neglect or abuse, genetic or biological causes, substance abuse, low self-esteem, personality disorder, or depression.

To Lie or Tell the Truth: Gain or Lose?

In the short term, telling lies to get ahead can seem like a great shortcut to what you want in life. However, in the long run, you will find yourself losing a lot. The thing about lies is that sooner or later, the truth will become evident. When that happens, everything you have gained by lying will begin to crumble.

If you make a habit of telling lies, you will find that you are actually pushing away the people who would be critical to your success. No one wants to work with someone they cannot trust. Your relationships also suffer because everyone you love has no choice but to second guess everything you say and do—and that is assuming they're still sticking around you since lying makes you look terribly selfish and unappealing. Everyone abhors being deceived, and so it is only a natural inclination to want to get as far away from a known liar as possible.

Make a habit of being honest as often as you can. When you stay honest, you do not have to worry about never fulfilling your promises. You won't have to worry about doing something wrong that contradicts your story. You don't have to feel terrible about all the lies you have told, or worry that you're not the person you have led others to believe you are.

You might want to assume that there is nothing to the "small" lies you tell, but if you keep that up, sooner or later, you are going to start lying about the bigger things too. The things you do every day—your habits—often sculpt the person you will become tomorrow. Lying is also an incredibly slippery slope. You go from telling constant white lies to telling more consequential lies, cheating, and stealing from other people. This is how the Bernie Madoffs of the world are created.

Honestly, honesty is just a lot easier since you do not have to try to remember whom you told what, or worry about the little inconsistencies that are inevitable with each version of your tall tales; inconsistencies that make it easy for everyone to wise up to your dishonesty and deception.

How to Lie or Hide the Truth

To spot the Machiavellian, it would befit you to get into their minds and see just how they can do what they do so well. For this reason, included in this section is what to look out for.

1. *You must lie only when needed.* Do not lie unless you have to—which means you have something to gain. That is the difference between a skilled liar and a pathological one. The pathological liar will tell so many lies, and often that's what lands them in hot water. The expert liar will tell the truth and nothing but the truth—unless and until they have something to gain from lying.

2. *Work out your story.* You want to make sure you have figured out your story before you lie. Do not wait until the last minute to figure things out, because if you do, then you're going to get caught. You want to make sure you have thought through your story and addressed every objection that can be raised. When you've rehearsed your lie enough times, it makes it more difficult to catch you out.

3. *Lie with the truth.* Rather than go with an outright lie, you must, at least, bend the truth. The best lies are those that do not really lie. You should tell the truth in a way that allows people to take on a different impression than the one you would rather they didn't have.

4. *Understand your target.* You need to get into your target's head. In other words, all good liars are good communicators. They are experts at tapping into other people's thoughts and feelings and reading them accurately. You must be empathetic to your target because it is easy to tell exactly what they want to hear from you, and you won't stick your foot in it. It's not enough to think of how sound the logic of a lie is to you. You must also make sure you consider the point of view of your target. That way, you can easily cover your tracks.

5. *Keep your story straight.* Lying is hard. You need to be consistent about the details. If you have to take notes, take notes. The trouble with terrible liars is that they tell different stories to different people. This can confuse the liar and increase the likelihood that people will start talking—and they'll figure it out. So, keep your story straight, no matter who is asking you about it.

6. *Stay sharp.* You must be focused. You must commit to the story you are telling. If you're accused of lying, do not allow yourself to feel guilt or fear. If you do, those emotions will show on your face and in your mannerisms—they're a dead giveaway. Commit to the story. A great way to commit is to flip a switch in your head by actively recalling your new story as if it is exactly what happened. Convince yourself you're not a liar, and no one else can convince you otherwise—even when you're smack dab in the middle of a lie. Enjoy the process of deception, of confusing your target. Whatever you do,

do not feel ashamed or remorseful. If you can enjoy misleading them, then you're not likely to slip up. Beware the dreaded duper's delight, though. You don't want that small, secret smile to slip onto your face unless you're actually telling a funny or happy story.

7. *No giveaways.* Do you want to be a great liar? Then you need to be aware of what you are signaling nonverbally. You want to keep eye contact, but no more or less than you usually do in a conversation. You want to keep your body language and palms open, as this subconsciously communicates that you have nothing to hide. Keep your breathing even. Don't swallow. Don't scratch. Don't fidget. Don't let your voice go lower or higher than usual, and be mindful not to gesture more than usual.

8. *Crank it up.* When your target suspects you are lying, you have got to raise the bar emotionally. All the great liars are amazing at manipulating people. Double down on emotion. Alternatively, ask them to set aside their feelings and look at things logically for a moment, and then walk them through your brand of logic. The fact that you're using the word "logic" with them already prompts them to assume whatever next will come out of your mouth is the truth and nothing but. You can also distract them. If you are incredibly attractive, and you're fairly certain that they cannot help but notice it, play that up to your advantage. If you are a 40-year-old with a babyface, you can appeal to them by subtly playing up childlike innocence, especially if it's someone who feels a need to be in a position above you all the time.

9. *Push back.* Most regular people are not okay with lying and are just as uncomfortable with pointing fingers at others. As a liar, you can use this to your advantage. Notice the way politicians will aggressively respond to the accusations made against them. This aggression is not necessarily always what it seems. With this aggression, they turn their targets away from the actual issue, so that they will have to regroup and have another go at accusing them—by this time, the politician will have sufficiently prepared for the next round of questions and accusations.

10. *Strike a deal.* Even if you are caught in a lie, you can escape the worst consequences by bargaining—as psychologists call it. What you want to do is reduce, soften, or totally eradicate all the feelings of responsibility for the lie you told. When you can reduce how accountable you are for the lies, as well as the anger and blame that result from your lies, you will be more likely to have an even better outcome than whatever lay in wait for you if you hadn't bargained.

Chapter Five: Learning Human Behavior

You cannot detect deception without understanding human behavior. This chapter details the various clues in human behavior that means deception is in play. While there are no specific clues that are exclusively tied to deception, there are clues that you can pay attention to regarding cognition and emotion.

For the most part, lies are often given away on account of the circumstances or factors around the lie, not necessarily by the liar's behavior. That said, sometimes behavior is all you have to go on to figure out whether or not you are being lied to about someone's actions or their intentions. Since the Machiavellian lies deliberately, it would not be a stretch to assume that there are some subtle signs in how they act that can give them away.

These are the questions that matter:

• Are there any clues that you can find when they tell lies?

• If there are clues, can you spot them with just your eyes, unassisted?

• Are these clues consistent all the time, regardless of the liar in question, the situation, or the culture in play?

- Assuming there are clues, is there a way to figure them out in real time, without using technology?

Wouldn't it be grand if every liar's nose magically grew an inch every time they told a lie? Unfortunately, this is not the case, and even science has not pinpointed a set of clues that apply to everyone, regardless of the situation and culture. The traditional clues of deception known to most folks, like fidgeting, stammering, avoiding eye contact, and so on, can happen for other reasons besides someone lying to you.

Learned Human Behaviors and Tics of a Liar

There is research on the detection of lies based on behavior, and you can broadly classify them into two categories:

- Cognitive clues involve the Machiavellian's memory and thoughts about what they are saying.
- Emotional clues involve the Machiavellian's feelings as they lie and their feelings around the subject of deception in general.

Cognitive Clues of Deception

There is a lot of effort that goes into the concealing, fabricating, or distorting information—much more effort than you would need simply to tell the truth. The Machiavellian will have to come up with stories about what did not actually happen, find ways to cover up what did happen and talk about things in such a way as to allow people to get whatever meaning they will out of their words.

There is also some effort involved in telling the truth when it is not exactly comfortable, as you'd need to find the most delicate way to put it so as not to offend the listener or make them feel bad. With telling uncomfortable truths, there are often clues, like more frequent disturbances in speech, the latency of speech, implausible or not so plausible ideas, much less involvement in terms of vocal and verbal communication, less time spent talking, and constant repetition of phrases and words, among other clues. The science also shows that there can be a change in nonverbal communication behaviors on account of all this effort. For instance, the usual hand and head movements that are made with speech will often give away when someone is lying versus telling the truth.

Another thing to consider when it comes to lies and cognition are the characteristics of naturalistic memory. When you have experienced an event, there are memory qualities, which are very clear as you describe those events, versus when you describe events that are not real. When you're telling a tall tale about something that never happened, your story often has more ambivalence and fewer details, and there is also no logical sequence of events, little to no plausibility a lot more in the way of negative statements, and less in the way of context.

The liar is not likely to admit to being forgetful, and they are not likely to make spontaneous adjustments or corrections to their stories. They may make more use of words describing negative emotions, and they also will do their best to distance themselves from the lie they're telling by referring to themselves as little as possible. The clues you can spot regarding the mental effort the liar uses appear to happen more as they deliver their lie. All clues about memory recall lie within the lie's context.

Be aware that not all lies require effort for everyone. Close-ended questions that require only "yes" or "no" answers are pretty easy to answer with a lie. An open-ended question that requires a liar to get into more detail is not as easy for them to answer if they intend to be dishonest. You can also expect that the cleverer the liar, the more persuasive they can be. This is especially so if they choose to use an event that actually did happen at some point in time as their alibi, rather than creating an entirely new one. For instance, they can tell you that they were doing their laundry at the time a crime happened when really, they only recall the day before—which is the actual day they did their laundry.

Emotional Clues

It is not uncommon for lies to cause emotions in the liar, from the expression of "duper's delight" at having successfully deceived someone to the anxiety and worry about getting caught, to feelings of immense guilt at having to lie about something. Typically, emotions will manifest in your facial expressions and the tone of your voice, and sometimes this is all you need to go on to reliably tell how someone feels at any given point in time.

Research shows that the facial expressions for specific emotions like contempt, anger, fear, happiness, disgust, distress, sadness, and surprise are universally recognized across all cultures and are pretty much the same worldwide. Depending on the stakes involved with the lie being told, there will often be more of these facial expressions and vocal tone changes. If it's a casual lie—meaning a lie most people tell all the time and without much thought—there won't be as much emotion in play.

Studies have also shown that a liar will often seem much more nervous than someone honest. They are not quite as pleasant concerning facial expressions. They speak with a higher pitch and a lot of tension, their pupils dilate, and they fidget. When the lie is about how feel, the liar will show how they're actually feeling in how they speak and the expressions on their face—regardless of how hard they try to cover up their emotions. Remember that while they will show these tells, they're very subtle and often brief.

The Liar's Targets

Again, lying happens every day. Many people tell lies, and often, it is really no picnic trying to work out when you're being played. Now, no one is exempt from being the sucker at any point in time, but the trouble is that some people are really easy to deceive and manipulate—in particular, people who are very:

1. Optimistic
2. Passive
3. Empathetic

The Empath

For the empath, there is no need to overthink when people seek support or help from them, or present themselves as vulnerable. The empath feels other people's joys and pains deeply, making them easy prey for the Machiavellian. They are incredibly adept at reading and sensing other people's emotions, and it is this remarkable skill that leaves them open to the Machiavellian's schemes. Not once does the empath assume that someone may be faking their tears. They just reach out to help and comfort them because that is who they are. Honestly, there's nothing wrong with being an empath as long as you're an empath who is careful.

The Passive or Naive

Those who are naive or passive are also pretty easy to fool as their thoughts are very simple, and they don't have enough judgment or experience to tell when they're being lied to. You would never catch them thinking twice when a liar puts one over them. To them, the world is a simple place, and there's no reason for anyone to want to complicate it by lying. So, when they're lied to, they don't even realize it.

The Optimist

Optimists are also vulnerable because they would rather assume the best of everyone. The trouble is: "everyone" also includes the liar. They look at the world through gold-tinted glasses. No matter how weird or disturbing a lie is, the optimist more likely than not will not notice it since they are often honest with others and themselves and expect that same honesty back. You can rest assured that it is an optimist who came up with the phrase "benefit of the doubt."

So, are you being targeted by liars? This might not necessarily be the case—yet you should still exercise some caution when dealing with seemingly duplicitous people. People who lie are not necessarily doing so to target anyone in particular. That being said, they will play it by ear, stay flexible, and switch tactics depending on who it is they're interacting with.

In other words, it is possible to be susceptible to the deception in their words, in theory. Also, just because it's easier to lie to certain personalities than others does not mean that everyone else is impervious to being had. A good rule of thumb would be to tread carefully when you are dealing with strangers, at least. This is not advocating that you embrace paranoia; it is simply suggesting that you exercise caution.

Chapter Six: Manipulation Tactics

The Machiavellian can do what they do by manipulating you both psychologically and emotionally. Psychological manipulation happens when the Machiavellian socially influences you to act differently—the way they would prefer. They manipulate to change other people's perceptions and use deceptive, devious, indirect, and immoral tactics. The whole point of manipulation is to get something at the expense of another person. In other words, manipulation is manipulation on account of the exploitation and underhandedness that is going on.

Social influence is not always a bad thing. For instance, if you had a smoking habit, and your doctor, family, and friends did their best to persuade you to quit, that would not necessarily be a bad thing in the end. They have nothing to gain from your quitting. In fact, you are the one who is going to benefit the most from giving in to their persuasion. In this case, you're not being manipulated, merely persuaded. Another key difference between persuasion and manipulation is that the former is fine as long as everyone respects that you do not have to do as you are asked, and you're not under duress or being forced to comply with the suggestions. You and you alone can accept what they're suggesting, or trash it.

Key Aspects of Manipulation

For the manipulator to manipulate, they have to:

1. Hide their evil intentions and act like they are friendly and harmless.

2. Know the various ways in which their target is psychologically vulnerable so that they can figure out the best manipulative tactics to use.

3. Be ruthless enough to have no issues with harming their target when necessary.

Here is how the Machiavellian operates when it comes to maintaining control of the people they manipulate:

1. *They use positive reinforcement.* They will praise you, be all charming—except said charm is really superficial—throw money at you, show fake sympathy, give you approval, apologize more than is needed, give you lavish gifts and attention, force their smiles and laughter, and also publicly recognize you for having done well.

2. *They also use negative reinforcement.* They will offer to get you out of a terrible situation if you agree to do what they want you to do.

3. *They use partial or intermittent reinforcement, both positive and negative.* When it is the former, they can encourage you to keep going with whatever they want you to do. When it's the latter, they have you feeling a lot of doubt and fear about doing what you want to.

4. *They will flat-out punish you.* That punishment will include silent treatment, yelling, nagging, swearing, intimidation tactics, guilt-tripping, crying, emotional blackmail, sulking, and acting like the victim.

5. *They will cause you trauma just one time.* They do this so that you learn to fall in line. They can use explosive anger, verbal abuse, and other forms of intimidation to show you that they're the top dog, and they will take no guff from you or anyone. When you have experienced their reproach once, you're more than likely to find ways not to upset the person doing the manipulating.

Manipulative Techniques

Technique #1: Lying by omission. The Machiavellian chooses to withhold the most vital aspects of the truth.

Technique #2: Lying by the commission. Here, the truth is skewed; however, you cannot tell when the liar is lying to you. Keep in mind that the Machiavellian is a master at deception, and lies often and subtly.

Technique #3: Rationalization. The Machiavellian will come up with some excuse for why they acted as they did, even though it was totally inappropriate.

Technique #4: Denial. They refuse to fess up about what they have done.

Technique #5: Diversion. They do not give you a straightforward answer. They'd rather evade it by changing the topic.

Technique #6: Minimization. This involves both rationalization and denial. The Machiavellian will continue to insist that what they did was not as terrible or dangerous as someone says. They're the ones quick to dismiss cutting remarks they make as "just jokes."

Technique #7: Guilt-tripping. The Machiavellian will tell you, "You don't care at all. You're so selfish! I don't blame you, though. It's only because you've got an easy life." These kinds of statements make you feel guilty, so you find you are always anxious, you doubt yourself all the time, and you're submissive when it comes to them.

Technique #8: Covert intimidation. The manipulator will deliberately get you defensive by making implied, subtle, indirect threats, veiled just enough for you to get the message, and for others to miss it.

Technique #9: Vilification. The Machiavellian is all about getting you defensive with this very powerful technique. Not only are you defensive, but they also do a good job of covering the intent of their message and go one step further: They make you—the actual victim— seem like the abuser when you decide to defend yourself.

Technique #10: Shaming. The Mach will be sarcastic as they put you down in the presence of others. This serves to up the ante when it comes to how much you and everyone else fears them, and it also makes you doubt yourself. The shaming technique is not always so obvious. Sometimes it is only in their tone of voice; other times, it's an angry, intense look. They might make rhetorical comments you cannot respond to with an ever so subtle dash of sarcasm. They can make you feel scared or ashamed for attempting to stand up to them. It's a great way to make their targets feel terrible.

Technique #11: Acting the victim. The Machiavellian is fine with making themselves seem like the long-suffering victim of someone else, or circumstance, just to get people to feel bad for them or reach out to them and strengthen their relationships. The trouble is that the victims often have an actual heart, and their love and care inevitably put an X on their back for the Machiavellian to take aim and fire.

Technique #12: Acting the servant. They will mask their selfish agenda in a way that makes it seem like a noble cause. They'll say things like, "Hey, I'm just doing my job," when in all honesty, they're just taking pleasure from treating you dreadfully or seeing you in pain.

Technique #13: Blaming others. The Mach will seek out scapegoats and in the subtlest of ways, so subtle that you would find it hard to spot it. They will project their thoughts onto you and make it look like you are in the wrong. Even when you catch them in their lies and expose them for who they are, they will still blame you for being gullible in the first place, as though they had no choice but to exploit and deceive you for being so open and trusting. The only time the manipulator is okay with accepting the blame is when they want to seem like they feel remorseful.

Technique #14: Pretending innocence. The Mach will try to make you think they did not mean to hurt you. They'll lie and say that they didn't do what you're accusing them of. They may even feign surprise and act indignant. When they do this, you will start to wonder if you actually experienced things as you did, or if you're losing your mind.

Technique #15: Pretending confusion. The Machiavellian will act stupidly as they have absolutely no clue what you are talking about. They will act like they're confused whenever you address a serious issue with them. They will do all they can to make you confused so that you wonder if your version of events is actually valid, or your sanity is slipping. They will point out certain key points, which they had in place, like contingency plans for just the occasion. They will also have made sure they have people who can back up their story, either innocently or with as much malevolent intent as the Machiavellian itself.

Technique #16: Bandwagon effect. The Machiavellian will make you submit by comforting you, saying that a lot of people have already done whatever you are doing, and so you might as well do it too. They'll say things like, "People just like you . . ." or "Everyone's doing it."

Technique #17: Anger as a weapon. The Machiavellian will use anger like a weapon, brandishing it as intensely as they can to shock you into a submissive state. It seems like they are angry, but they're not. It is all an act. They want what they want from you, and they know that if they act angry, chances are you'll give it to them. They can manipulate you with controlled anger so that they do not have to deal with the embarrassment of a confrontation between you both, or they can hide their real intentions, or they can keep the truth hidden. They'll threaten to call the cops or threaten to make false reports.

Along with controlled anger, you get blackmail. The Machiavellian uses anger to avoid having to tell the truth when they don't want to. They use anger as a shield or defense mechanism so that all suspicions and inquiries are dead on arrival.

Real-World Examples of Manipulation

Meredith was concerned for her close friend Kayla. Kayla had a boyfriend named Jeff, who would always threaten her with suicide each time she tried to break up with him. She had very valid reasons to leave because he was verbally, physically, and sexually abusive. Finally, Meredith convinced Kayla to seek professional help, and in time, Kayla worked up the guts to end things with Jeff. He tried to threaten suicide to get her to stay again, but this time around, Kayla didn't give in. He was finally put on suicide watch, and Kayla made sure to block him from ever contacting her again. Threatening suicide is one thing manipulators do to keep people in line.

Ben had to deal with a manipulator at work who would never stick to the facts and would always accuse him of one thing or the other. One day, Ben had enough.

His boss had summoned him to the office and said, "You're disrespectful!"

Where Ben would ordinarily cower, this time around, he asked her, "How was I disrespectful?"

His boss was speechless, and this only made her livid. "I don't know, and I don't care! All I know is that you're incredibly disrespectful!"

So, Ben tried again by asking, "Who was I disrespectful to? Tell me, and I'll make it right." However, his boss had no concrete answer. It became pretty obvious his boss only wanted to manipulate him and bait him into reacting emotionally, but Ben had foiled her plans.

Ben pressed further by asking, "What have you heard me say or seen me do that makes you feel I'm disrespectful?"

His boss could do nothing but stutter in response. She never bothered him again.

Nigel had a relationship with Anita for two years, and he suffered unspeakable trauma. Anita would always take every chance she could to tell Nigel he did not remember things right, or that he had forgotten how things actually played out. As if this were not enough trouble for Nigel, he had schizoaffective disorder, which meant he had altered states and memory lapses. Nigel eventually figured out what was going on when he started speaking with other people going through the same thing. Once Anita had won an argument with him, she would make Nigel question his sanity and memory. She would swoop in and act like the angel, the good woman who was so forgiving and loving toward her broken boyfriend. She would remind him repeatedly that no matter what anyone had to say about it, she would never judge Nigel for his memory lapses.

Charles's ex-wife Lucy was well aware that he wanted a PS4 when the game console was released. It was all he could talk about. So, when Lucy wanted to do something, and she was well aware Charles would not enjoy at all, she would call him up on the phone while he was at work to let him know there was a surprise waiting for him at home. Days before she made that phone call, she would make subtle hints about the PS4 to Charles, and he would have it in mind. When she did call, she would do so several times to get him really excited by how amazing the surprise is, and how she could not wait for him to have it.

Charles would fall for it each time. He would arrive home, and there she'd be, proudly presenting him with some cheap necklace or a vest that she knew Charles would hate. She would watch him like a hawk, looking for a reaction that said he did not enjoy the gift. Once she realized he was extremely disappointed, she would start in with the crocodile tears.

"You don't like it? I don't believe it! Do you have any idea how much this cost? How long I had to wait to get it? You are incredibly insensitive and so ungrateful! You have no idea just how to hurt I feel right now!"

And on and on, she would go, accusing Charles of not being appreciative of her efforts. Inevitably, Charles would feel guilty, and then he would have to do whatever it was Anita wanted to placate her.

The second Charles gave Anita whatever it was she wanted the most, she would suddenly not care one bit about the "gift" she had gotten him. In fact, he actually wore one of the vests she'd gotten him once, and she had asked him, "Oh my goodness . . . Where did you get that hideous thing?"

Charles says Anita was a compulsive liar and a great manipulator— except when she hit the bottle.

Chapter Seven: Dark Negotiation Tactics

Negotiation is the process of coming to a mutually beneficial agreement. It often involves coming to a compromise or an understanding while making sure to avoid disputes and arguments. For some reason, many people are frightened about negotiating when there is really nothing to it other than striking a bargain—or at least, that is all it should be. The trouble happens when you're negotiating with someone who is Machiavellian or part of the dark triad. In this situation, it's easy to feel intimidated because they're actually experts at getting you to do whatever they want you to do, and unlike other normal people, they're not afraid to use dirty tricks and throw their weight around till you cower and hand over whatever they're asking for.

The Machiavellian and Dark Negotiation

In dark negotiation, there is no consideration for a win-win scenario. Even when it seems that way on the outset, you will find in the end that you have been shortchanged. Ethics or morals do not bind the Machiavellian, and so they are not afraid to play the negotiation game as low and as dirty as possible. So, it would be in your best interest to learn the kinds of tactics they use to coerce you into a position you'd really rather not be in.

Dark Negotiation Tactics

Tactic #1: *Fake disappointment.* The Machiavellian knows how powerful it is to act disappointed. It's not just anecdotal; science also backs this up. Research has shown that when you seem disappointed during negotiations, fewer demands are made of you, and more concessions are made to you. The reason for this is that the other person will feel the need to give you more to put you both on equal footing or make you feel better about the deal you're striking.

The Machiavellian is well aware of the power of acting disappointed. In fact, they will go so far as acting like they do not like the offer you've given them when, in all honesty, they could be ecstatic about what they've gotten out of you so far. The Machiavellian knows two things:

1. If they act unhappy, it's possible for them to be happier than they already are since they can ask for more.

2. If they act happy, it might make you think you should offer even less, or you should think twice about your offer to them.

The best negotiators—and Machiavellians—know never to take the first thing they're offered. They also know this: Never show you're impressed.

Block: When the Machiavellian acts unhappy, let them know that, unfortunately, there's not much else you can offer them, but if they let you know what it is they want, you can pass it along to the head honcho or a higher authority.

Tactic #2: "You're gonna have to do better than that." The pro negotiator or Machiavellian—these are not necessarily the same— knows to use the phrase. Then they stay silent and allow you to come forward and make a concession that works for them.

Block: When you hear that line, you must respond by asking something to the effect of, "Okay. How much better are we talking?"

When you answer this, you remain in charge of the negotiation. You also avoid making the mistake of going over and beyond what they really want from you.

Tactic #3: "*Don't be so defensive.*" When you hear this one, know that the manipulator is using reverse psychology on you. Often, this line will come up when the Machiavellian is well aware that you are not playing ball with them. If they sense you don't trust them, they'll ask you not to be so defensive, and they might follow that line up with a joke to get you to let your guard down. If you laugh or smile good-naturedly, it means you're going along with them, agreeing that yes, you are being too defensive, and you need to be more willing to make some more concessions.

Block: Do not ever respond by saying you're not defensive. If you do that, you will find yourself psychologically primed into acting more trusting, open, and trustworthy just to prove to them that they are wrong, and this puts the power right in their hands. Instead, you should say something like this: "Your method in dealing with me is making me defensive. If you want to get into that, I'll tell you precisely how and why." Replying this way puts the power squarely in your hands. On the other hand, you can simply reply with a joke like, "Offer me a better deal, and I'll put my sword and shield down." Make sure to smile, but in a way that doesn't reach your eyes. As you do, make sure you hold their gaze. Whatever you do, never look away, and never blink till they concede or change tactics.

Tactic #4: *Create a non-existent higher authority that makes it tough to concede.* How can you tell you are negotiating with an idiot? When they put themselves forward as the last bus stop or final authority. If the person you're negotiating with lets you know they have some "leeway for agreeing on a price," they don't have any power. The powerful negotiator knows to act like their nothing but an errand boy, a lamb, a mouthpiece. They act like they couldn't possibly decide all by themselves, and they'll need to check with the head honchos to figure out whether or not they can make the concessions you seek. With this non-existent leverage, they can play all sorts of games with you. They also have the advantages of:

1. Buying time while they "ask" their "people."

2. Seeming tough without being nasty about it. (They can claim they'd give you what you want, but they've got really tough bosses.)

3. Playing the last-minute agreement or concession trick on you (which will be detailed later in the book).

Block: There are several ways you can deal with this dark negotiation tactic:

1. Act as if you believe them while keeping in mind what game they're playing with you.

2. You can say, "Hey now, are we really playing good cop, bad cop?"

3. You can also say, "Great! When are you going to meet with them? I'd love to be there so I can talk with them too."

4. Or you can say, "Oh come on, you're the boss/expert/head honcho. I bet the others will have to go with your decisions anyway, don't they?"

Tactic #5: *Wrestle a last-minute agreement with fake last-minute snags.* It is not uncommon for the manipulator to wait until the last minute to tell you, "Something just came up." They do this to get a last-minute concession out of you.

At first, everything goes swimmingly well. In fact, they have greenlit the transaction, and they let you know they just need to check in with the boss or the board, and it all sounds like it's a solid, done deal. However, at the last minute, they come back to you to let you know the board or the boss is being difficult, and so you have no choice but to make a concession.

Block: When they let you know that the people in charge are difficult, let them know you will also need to get back to your people, or you are going to have to think over what they're telling you. If you're in a situation where they need you a lot more than you need them, you should go ahead and exploit that. You can say, "Look, Joe, I thought long and hard about this, and I really would like to hold on to my end of the bargain. But I've had time to crunch the numbers, and every day I'm busier and busier with more demand, and . . . I hate to have to go back on my word, but considering the way the market is, I've got to charge you ten percent more for it to be worth my while. Now, since I gave you a much different price than this, I'm willing to cut that down to five percent, but only for you. So, let me know by the end of the day."

Tactic #6: *Good cop, bad cop.* You already know how this one goes. Here are the different ways this can play out:

1. The bad cop acts strictly while the good cop acts more agreeable.

2. The bad cop acts enraged and storms out of the room, while the good cop acts like a friend.

3. The good cop lets you know they'd give you what you're asking for, but the powers that be—also known as "bad cop"—won't let them.

Block: Have your very own bad cop, real or fake. Alternatively, you can act like you're falling for their ruse, and then use it to your advantage so you can see what it is they offer you. When the person acting as the good cop offers you a deal, they will have shown you their hand. They've automatically let you know what works for them—which is what you must absolutely not accept.

Tactic #7: *Let them come to you.* When it comes to negotiations, the perceived power is very important. The more power you have, the more concessions you get in a negotiation because the weaker negotiator is forced to give you what you want. Here are some subtle ways in which the negotiator can demonstrate power over you:

- Come over to my office (or home, or their preferred location.)
- I am only free from 7 AM to 7:30 AM, is that good for you?
- I am quite busy this week. Let's talk next week, all right?

When you can avoid it, do not go to their home or office, or wherever they want you to meet. If you meet them on their turf, it basically says that they have more power. It also makes them feel much more secure, which means they have the advantage.

Block: Propose your preferred location, or ask them to meet you halfway. Another thing you should never do is chase them too hard—unless you are willing to give your power away, or it is part of your long-term strategy.

Tactic #8: *Encirclement.* This involves being outnumbered. The start of negotiations is often a tug of war, where the game is about holding on to the most power. The way these tactic works is simple—the negotiator shows up with a bunch of other people, and that can make you feel automatically defensive. If you notice that they are all sitting on one side of the table, or worse, all around you, they're basically trying to frame the situation into a "many versus one" situation. In case it is just you and two other people negotiating, be mindful if one of them sits opposite you while the other chooses to sit by your side. They might be springing for the good cop versus bad cop game.

Block: You should say to them, "I expected only Joe. Why are you here with more friends?" The negotiator might reply, "They're actually also interested, and they had time to join us, so now we're here, let's sit down and talk, shall we?" In this case, you should respond, "Rather than try to play negotiation games, let's come up with a win-win solution. Okay?"

If you are unafraid of seeming really bold, and you know for a fact there is absolutely no need for other people to be involved in the negotiation, you can try saying this: "Listen, I've been in contact with you, Joe, and if it's not too much trouble, I'd rather talk with just one person. The more people involved, the more it gets complicated. I'd rather keep it as simple as possible." Then add, while staring at the other uninvited people, "I know a great place in the area I can recommend to you guys where you can grab drinks and great food."

Tactic #9: *Nibbling—or the "last drops" technique.* Say you are done negotiating and so close to signing papers. You can finally relax and maybe even spend time socially with your negotiator for some beer. Now, you let your hair down, and you're excited about wrapping things up. Just as you go out to celebrate, the Machiavellian or pro negotiator will do their best to milk you for some concessions or get the "last drops" of champagne out of you.

They may say, "By the way, you're going to write bonus material for the book, right?" If your response is "no" or that the time is not right to tack on any more clauses to your agreement, they will do their best to make it seem like it was already obvious that you would have to do what they're asking. They might do this by saying, "Oh, come on now. The only reason we didn't talk about it is that's the standard procedure. Everyone's got to agree to write bonuses."

Block: You have to control the frame. You can do this by saying, "No, that isn't right. You claim everyone's got to, but who's everyone? In my experience, no one does, and no one asks for that. So, don't try to mess things up when we've already come to a great arrangement for us both."

Here are other ways you can deal with it:

- Smile like they are just joking.
- Let them know that the deal they already have is pretty awesome as it stands, and that's the end of it.
- Let them know that after that dark move they just pulled, dinner, after the papers are signed, is on them. But, if they are quick enough to get you to sign, you might be nice enough to still celebrate with them. Then offer a sweet smile and wait.

Tactic #10: *Flinch at First Sight.* A great negotiator will be quick to "flinch" when you make your first offer. It is a powerful nonverbal response that says, "Are you nuts? Cut that number way, way down, right now!" If you come down right away, you are no longer in a position of power and will lose all credibility.

The flinch could be a dramatic shout as they repeat your offer back to you, or it could be as subtle as them taking a step back and sighing. More often than not, a good negotiator will choose not to go the dramatic route, as that is a great way to ruin the rapport and comes off as insulting toward you and the product you're offering.

Rather than get loud, they might pause and seem flustered and thoughtful, almost like they are saying, "I really want this, but that price is too crazy!" Then they might compliment you and try to hype you up as they execute the flinch. It could be something like this: "Well, I get why you want to get paid that much. I mean, it's you. Your work speaks for itself, and I'm a huge fan. I would really love to work out a way to work with you." They're building rapport and buttering you up to make you softer so you can drop your price and not lose face. A terrible negotiator would try to make you or your service seem worthless.

Block: Never go back on your first offer straightaway. If you do, you are done. Instead, you should ask what it is they are thinking, and when they offer you their deal, you should flinch in response too. If they're buttering you up, you can simply reply, "Thank you. I'd really love to work with you, too, so I really hope somehow you can figure out a way to pay the proper and fair price, so we can get started immediately."

There are many games the dark negotiator plays. Keep your eyes wide open.

Chapter Eight: Persuasion Techniques and Principles

Persuasion is all about influencing other people's attitudes, motivations, beliefs, behaviors, and intentions. When it happens in business, it is about changing the attitude of a group or a person toward an object, or an idea, or other people or groups, while making use of visual tools, spoken and written words, and whatever else will help to pass along feelings, reasonings, and information in general. It's also about making use of your resources, both personal and positional, to have people thinking or behaving the way you would like them to.

You can either opt for systematic persuasion, where you change attitudes and behaviors by appealing to reason and logic or go for heuristic persuasion, where you appeal to people's emotions or habits to get them to swing your way.

The 21 Principles of Persuasion

You have probably wondered how it is that some people are incredibly persuasive. How do they get so skilled at getting others to see things their way? Well, the following 21 principles will help you learn to be persuasive and spot when a Machiavellian is in the process of persuading you so that you can keep your guard up.

#1: *Persuasion and manipulation are two different things.* Manipulation involves being coerced to do something that is definitely not in your best interests. On the flip side, persuasion is about getting people to do things that will benefit them in the long run—and benefit you.

#2: *Only ever try to persuade those who can be persuaded.* Sure, you can persuade everyone, but only when the timing and the context are right. However, just because everyone can be persuaded does not mean that they can be persuaded right away. Many political campaigns spend a lot of their money and time on just a small group of swing voters who usually determine the winner of an election. There is a reason for that. So, the first thing you want to do is figure out who, at a certain time, can be persuaded to see things your way. Then, give them all of your attention and energy.

#3: *The timing and context matter.* These two things are fundamental to the art of persuasion. It is the context that gives a baseline for what is okay. The timing is what sets the tone for what you want from other people and life. You would rather marry someone different from the sort of person you dated in your younger years because your wants and needs naturally change over time. Just because the person you want to persuade wanted something yesterday doesn't mean they are still desperate to have it today.

#4: *Only those who are interested can be persuaded.* You cannot persuade someone who does not care about what you are offering them. For the most part, no one cares about you. They only care about number one—themselves. Everyone's thoughts are preoccupied with health, money, or love. To persuade people, you need to understand how to talk to them about themselves. If you learn to keep the spotlight on them, they will keep their eyes and ears focused on you.

#5: *Reciprocity is a compelling force.* For some reason, when someone does something for you, you feel the need to do something for them. It is hardwired in people's brains that they should help others to thrive. You—or the Machiavellian—can use this need to reciprocate to persuade other people. When you offer small, meaningful gestures to others, you automatically can ask for a lot more from them in return—and they'll be happy to help you.

#6: *Be persistent.* It pays. Whoever is able and willing to continue to ask for the things they want, and continues to offer value consistently, is often the most persuasive person. For this reason, many historical leaders have been able to rally the masses to be on their side.

#7: *Be sincere in your compliments.* Everyone loves sincere compliments. Something about them puts a pep in one's step. People tend to trust those who make them feel good. So, putting two and two together, it becomes obvious that when you can, you should compliment other people. Be sincere, and even better, compliment things about them that they are not usually praised for. When you offer sincere compliments, it is much easier to persuade other people.

#8: *Set concrete expectations.* A huge part of persuasion is effectively managing other people's expectations so they can trust your choices. Say you are a CEO, and you promise to rake in twenty percent more in sales, but you pull in thirty percent more—you will definitely be rewarded. However, if you promise 40 percent, but you pull in only 37, you're sure to get punished. In other words, make sure you underpromise and overdeliver.

#9: *Never assume.* Do not think you know what it is the next person needs. Just make your value plain. Unfortunately, especially in the world of sales, many people will not bother to offer their service or products because they make the erroneous assumption that others don't have any interest or don't have the money to pay. Never assume what people want. Just make your offer and let them decide.

#10: *Manufacture scarcity.* The value of everything is relative. People tend to want things because other people want these things. When you want someone to want what you have, you must make that thing scarce—even when you are the object of desire.

#11: *Manufacture urgency.* You must make the people you are persuading feel like they need to make a decision and act immediately. If they are not driven enough to want something from you right away, chances are they won't be driven in the future either. You must persuade the people in the here and now, and you can do this by playing up the urgency or inducing FOMO—the fear of missing out.

#12: *Pictures are potent.* More potent than what you hear is what you see. That is the reason you watch a commercial for a drug, where the setting is a happy place with smiling people, while in a low tone and superfast, there's a voice-over talking about the drug's deadly side effects. Pictures say a lot more than words. So, you must be willing to give a great first impression in the minds of the people you're persuading.

#13: *Tell the truth.* If you want to persuade someone, you should tell them stuff about themselves that no one else will say. There is nothing more meaningful than being confronted with the hard truth about you. When you tell people the truth, with no agenda and no judgment, not only will people respect you more, but they'll also be more open to being persuaded.

#14: *Establish rapport.* For some reason, people like others who are similar to themselves. This affects every decision they make, consciously and subconsciously. When you mirror and match other people's behaviors, including patterns of speech, body language, speech cadence, and so on, it is easy to create rapport with others so that they are more comfortable being around you, and therefore more open to your suggestions.

#15: *Be flexible in your behavior.* Often, the person who has control over the situation or interaction is the one who is the most flexible, not the person who's wielding the most power. Many children are extremely persuasive because they are willing to run through the whole gamut of all the behaviors they need to get what they want. They will be charming, pout, bargain, cry, plead—whatever they have to do. While as a parent, all you can do is say "no." You should have a collection of behaviors you can resort to. That way, you will be much more persuasive.

#16: *Become a master of energy transference.* There are people whom you spend time with who leave you completely drained. In contrast, others pump you full of energy. The people who are the most persuasive are masters at infusing others with energy. They transfer their energy to others to fire them up and get them feeling motivated. They do this using physical touch, eye contact, laughter, excitement in their speech, or just listening actively.

#17: *Be clear in your communication.* You must explain your ideas and point of view so that even a kid could get it. If you can't, it is way too complicated. If you are going to be persuasive, you have to keep things as simple as possible and make sure to communicate the core meaning of whatever idea you're trying to pass along.

#18: *Preparation puts you way ahead.* You must make sure that you are well aware of whom you're dealing with and the circumstances. When you do your best to be ready, you will effectively persuade others. For instance, if you learn everything you can about a prospective employer and their services, products, and background, chances are you will be more than prepared for an interview, and you will most likely land the gig.

#19: *Be detached and calm in conflict.* When tempers are flying all around you, it helps to keep a level head. When you are the one who remains on tilt, you will also be the one in control. You must learn to keep your cool, remain calm and detached, and forget your emotions for the time being. When there is conflict, it is to you that people will turn to. It is you that people will trust, and you will be right there to lead them where they need to go.

#20: *Be deliberate in your anger.* It is a rare person who is at peace with conflict. If you want to increase the level of conflict and tension in a situation, most others want the opposite and would rather back down. You can use this to your advantage but do so sparingly. Whatever you do, don't do it out of a lack of self-control or from an emotional position. Just keep in mind that you can use anger as a tool to get people to go along with your vision.

#21: *Be certain and confident.* There is nothing quite as attractive as being confident in who you are and your decisions. When you are sure of yourself, other people find it intoxicating and compelling. They will be more than willing to do as you ask. If you truly buy into what you do, it will take little to nothing to get others to do what would serve them while you get what you want from them as well.

Persuasion vs. Manipulation

Every day, people persuade other people. Each time, it is because they have a vested interest in getting them to do what they would like them to do. There is nothing wrong with persuasion; it's a natural part of human interaction. You can think of it from an altruistic point of view, as you'd like to see a better world, and so you persuade people to act better or hold better beliefs that would foster that sort of world.

It could be that you are just trying to make some money. There is nothing immoral with making money. That said, the people you're trying to persuade to buy from you are looking for reasons to hold on to their money. You have to let them know why they should agree to part with their money and what is in it for them if they hand it over.

Manipulation is using deceitful, unfair, and artful methods to influence others to serve your selfish goals. The thing about manipulation is that it never leads to a win-win scenario. The manipulator is only out for themselves. This is the key difference between persuasion and manipulation. The former seeks mutual benefit or the benefit of others; the latter seeks selfish gain.

If you ever find yourself wondering what you are doing—persuading someone or manipulating them—you only need to ask yourself, "What's in it for the other person?" If you cannot honestly come up with something that benefits them, but you have no problems coming up with all the ways influencing them would benefit you, you are being manipulative.

Manipulation might work in the interim, but it always leaves a wake of dissatisfaction. People sooner or later get sick of the Machiavellian's antics, and their outcry and rage become too intense to sweep under the rug. So, in the end, it is much better to persuade people. It's better to let them have their own reasons for joining your cause, as these reasons are genuine, and the people are intrinsically motivated. The trouble with extrinsic motivation is that it's pretty easy to drop—especially when they realize you are a manipulator who never actually follows through with their promises. Unlike you, a Machiavellian has no noble intentions. They do not merely persuade; they manipulate. You never have to worry about whether or not you are doing right by other people, as long as you make a point of seeking out scenarios where everybody wins and is happy. Seek the greater good for all involved, and paradoxically you will garner all the support you need—from everyone who knows you—to achieve your lofty ideals.

Chapter Nine: Non-Verbal Deception

To talk about nonverbal deception, you must get into nonverbal communication. There are other ways people communicate with each other besides actually speaking, and these methods altogether make up nonverbal communication. Nonverbal communication is just as important as the stuff people say, as it lends much more context and richness of meaning to whatever they are saying or hearing. The trouble is, in this day and age, people are so used to doing a lot of business over the phone or using emails so much that a good number of people are starting to lose touch with the nuances that are a part of face-to-face conversations. It is important to check this because, in the end, nothing beats a live connection with other people.

Albert Mehrabian, a psychologist and also the author of the bestselling book *Silent Messages: Implicit Communication of Emotions and Attitudes*, has conducted research on the matter of nonverbal communication and discovered that with all messages, only about seven percent of meaning is passed on through words, while the remaining 93 percent is passed on through silent, nonverbal communication—and more often than not, the nonverbal communication says much more than words ever could.

Ways People Communicate Nonverbally

Facial expression: This is very common and revealing. Look in a mirror. The face staring back at you can make over 10,000 various expressions, with each one giving tones of meaning and info easily. Frowning, smiling, blinking, and rolling your eyes are expressions that are relatable and strong. Flaring your nostrils or twitching your eyebrows are expressions that also convey meaning with no effort. If you want to connect with someone you do not know, all you have to do is smile at them! When you do, you are welcoming them, setting a warm frame, and making it so that the other person wants to spend time with you.

Body movement (also called kinesics): Body movement includes hand gestures and nodding. With your body, you can let people know you are excited about something. Think of the woman or man who loves to gesture wildly with their hands. There are other aspects of kinesics, too, like the stuff people would associate with anxiety—clearing your throat, trembling, or shaking your leg. When you're in a meeting, you want to make sure your hands are on the table or gently clasped together. Don't keep touching your face, or drumming on the table or your thigh, because these things are not only distracting but can communicate that you're not paying attention.

Posture: Posture is how you hold your body, which often makes a strong and lasting impression on people. The way you sit or stand is critical when it comes to how people perceive you. If you stand with your back straight and your head held high, it says you are strong, confident, and screams assurance in volumes. If you slouch or look to the ground, it says you're weak, uncertain, and perhaps indifferent. If you want to show people that you're friendly, keep your posture open. You want to stand with both legs hip-width apart, keeping your torso open rather than covering it by crossing your arms. Your head should be held high, and your face should be relaxed. When you cross your arms in a closed posture, you're telling people you do not want to be approached, or, at best, bored, and at worst, hostile.

Eye contact: You would be hard-pressed to find a better way to establish rapport with strangers than by holding eye contact. When you maintain eye contact, it means you are paying attention. You're interested and involved. If you do not hold eye contact, it could be read as you being rude, disinterested, or distracted. Holding eye contact does not mean you should stare right into their face—that is actually an intimidation tactic. You want to look sort of randomly around their eyes, including the eyebrows and eyelids.

Paralanguage: This involves the parts of verbal communication that have nothing to do with words and affect the meaning of the words being said. If you have ever had to tell a petulant teen, "Don't take that tone with me," you know exactly what this refers to—things like sarcasm, where the tone of their voice does not match what they're saying. For instance, someone saying "How thrilling" in a less than thrilling tone of voice is clearly not thrilled—and you got that from their tone, not the words themselves. Or if someone makes a presentation and the whole time they just mumble as quickly as they can, it could let you know that they're disingenuous or just nervous. On that note, be aware of how fast you talk. Make sure you speak up and clearly so that everyone can hear you. This doesn't mean you should get too loud, though, because not only does it seem belligerent and uncouth, it's also off-putting.

Proxemics: Proxemics is all about how close or far away someone is when you talk to them. You may have heard the term "close talker." For the most part, people are very aware and protective of their private, personal space—also called the "intimate space" by Mehrabian. This space is typically about six to eight inches. This zone is only ever for close friends, family, and romantic partners. When you are talking business at work, often you will be much further than that from the other people—just far away enough that everyone's comfortable, but not too far to seem uninterested or like you're deliberately distancing yourself.

Physiological changes: Emotions are closely linked to nonverbal communication. You will find that you have the most physiological responses when you're feeling uncomfortable or anxious. Blushing, flushing, sweating, itchy armpits, and tears in your eyes make it obvious that you're not feeling so great right now. When you notice that someone you're talking to is not feeling okay or is nervous, you should do what you can to make them feel at ease. You can often tell from the pitch of their voice and the clamminess of their palms when you shake them whether or not they're nervous.

Nonverbal Deception

Because the Machiavellian is well aware that their body language can give them away, they are careful to act in congruent ways with the lies that they're spinning you. The way the body responds to big lies is often dependent on the liar's fear that they will be discovered or something will give them away, and they will have to deal with major consequences. Research has shown that the expectations surrounding how a liar acts when they're lying are wrong—whether those expectations are of the layperson or professional interrogators. You cannot just see someone sweating bullets and assume they're telling a lie. Maybe it is hot, or they really need to go to the bathroom.

When some people lie, they look you in the eye. Others do not. Some will look frozen, and others will move about like a motivational speaker. They might look one way when they are trying to put one over you and look the same way when they're not. They can deliberately set up their nonverbal cues to seem like they're honest.

The fact is you may be able to see nonverbal behavior, but you can only guess what each behavior means or what is causing it. Just because someone is nervous during an interview does not mean that the interview is the problem. It also does not mean they're lying—perhaps it's their first interview. The way to take a look at nonverbal behavior and deception is to look at the behavior more as an alert or a cause for concern, or a clue that you might want to ask more questions to gauge the actual cause of the problem.

Nonverbal Deception Cues

While you cannot and should not make assumptions about whether someone is lying based on these cues alone, you should know what to look out for to press the issue at hand further and get to the truth.

Gestures can let you know when you are being lied to. Studies show that liars will often gaze downwards and move their heads and hands in a faster or slower way than usual. Again, you should never use nonverbal cues to detect deception. What you want to do is use them to detect stress, which can help you ask the right questions of the person in question.

Anti-gravity signals are something the liar will also give. According to Joe Navarro, an FBI special agent, the liar will often use gestures that defy gravity, like lifting themselves onto their toes when they are standing, often at the end of their sentence, to make their point clearer. Or they raise their toes when they're seated. Another thing they do is raise their eyebrows, which means they trust the words they are spinning.

The palm-up gesture often gives a clue about deception. It shows inability or helplessness. The hand shrug gesture also shows up as a sort of nonverbal slip, letting you know they may not be as honest as they seem.

There is also the self-touch, where the suspected liar will put their hand to their face subconsciously to cover their shame over being deceitful. They might do this by covering their eyes or touching their forehead, all while gazing downward.

When it comes to nonverbal deception, certain changes happen in six categories regarding behavior:

1. Changes that show underlying anxiety.

2. Changes that show withdrawal.

3. Excessive attitudes and displays that do not match with the liar's usual response when they are honest.

4. Changes that show there is a covert negative affect.

5. Changes that show uncertainty and vagueness.

6. Changes that show mixed messages or incongruous responses.

The Power of Nonverbal Cues

Nonverbal cues are much more powerful than words or actions. Within just moments of meeting someone, they will have formed their impression of you, even if they really have no idea who you are. They'll have taken into account your dressing, comportment, and how your body talks. It is just the way human interaction goes.

If you want to make sure that you are hardly ever the victim of deceit, you need to become a human nonverbal communication scholar. The reason is simple: Your body and gestures will often give away a lot more than your words. The same is true for a Machiavellian, and knowing this can help you stay one step ahead of the game.

Nonverbal communication is a great way for you to spot the lack of congruence between what someone tells you and what they really think or feel. The ability to read people skillfully will also keep you from embarrassing situations and losses. Whenever something does not quite feel right, it is often hard for most people to hide that from others, especially if they are close to you. When they do try, what happens more often than not is inevitable conflict and misunderstanding. Nonverbal communication is vital because it is often done unconsciously, meaning it's out of the deceiver's control. So, nonverbal cues are a great way to ascertain an issue not being handled or disclosed as fully as it should be.

Nonverbal cues are also important in therapy as they can provide the therapist with insight into their patients. If the therapist or counselor is well aware of their patient's nonverbal cues and can weigh them against the words they say, they can decide whether or not there is a match between them. It is safe to say that the therapist, more often than not, will learn a lot more from what is not said than from what is being said, and armed with this info, they will find the deeper issues that plague their patients—who may not even be aware of them.

In fact, there is somatic experiencing, which is a kind of therapy that is especially helpful in treating people who deal with trauma. It considers the physical responses and body language of the person undergoing treatment as the counselor or therapist introduces them to the cause of their trauma in small, safe doses. The therapist then deciphers the nonverbal cues to assess where their patient is at regarding recovery.

Nonverbal cues are further significant in body-mind psychotherapy, where the patient's sounds, breaths, and body movements are measured. This is so the therapist can easily pinpoint the patient's behaviors that are counterproductive and then help them develop new, better habits to replace the old behaviors. If you want to get better at reading nonverbal cues, you must observe people around you. Compare and contrast their reactions and behaviors when they speak with you at certain times about specific issues versus other times and other issues. With your eyes open, you will see what is really going on.

Chapter Ten: Who Uses These Tactics?

Manipulation or Deception?

Say you are a salesperson. You are tasked with one job: Getting the prospect to exchange their money for what you're selling. That is a tough thing to do since people are always looking for good reasons not to buy. To get rid of the natural desire to say "no," you would have to resort to certain tactics as a marketer or salesperson.

- You might put up a sign that says, "50% off!"
- Or "2-day sale!"
- Or "Only 7 more left!"

When you use signs like this, your prospect goes from arguing against buying it to thinking it is such a great deal that they would have to be stupid to let it go. These tactics of urgency, scarcity, and exclusivity work very well as you tap into the buyer's lizard brain and get them actually to do something about it. These tactics are persuasion levers, and many people get uncomfortable at the thought of using them because they consider them manipulative. They have a point; it is manipulative. Getting people to swipe their cards is calculating, but it is definitely not the same as deception. So, if you work in sales, or you have ever found yourself in a situation where you had to use these tactics, and you feel gross about it, it's probably because you are assuming manipulation and deception are the same things.

Manipulation is great when you want people to take action. It is using skillful persuasion to get someone to take action concerning their interests. Again, you can only persuade people who are interested in what you are offering—and since everyone only cares about themselves, they're probably interested because they know what you're offering could be good for them. All you're doing is letting them know why they should not just get it but get it right now.

This being said, some salespeople do not care about making claims that are unsubstantiated if it means it will bring them sales.

People Who Use Deceptive Tactics

There are certain industries where liars thrive. Salespeople have already been discussed, so who else is suspect when it comes to deception?

Congress members are not considered the most honest people on account of their wheeling and dealing. There is no surprise that this is the general perception of people in politics as a whole.

Lobbyists, for obvious reasons, are not very honest. You can expect a fair number of them to have Machiavellian traits—if they are not outright Machiavellians—since they need to do what they must to get people to swing their way.

Car salespeople are not generally trusted because people often tend to get the short end of the stick when dealing with them. In fact, according to a Gallup poll, only seven percent of Americans think that car salespeople can be trusted.

Telemarketers do not have a lot of fans. At best, people consider them a nuisance; at worst, they have a propensity to conflate figures, tell tales, and say whatever they need to in order to make you give up your credit card details.

Stockbrokers have a long way to go before they can be considered honest, particularly as the industry is often rife with unethical practices like insider trading and things of that nature. It is a pretty cutthroat industry that often only attracts people who can handle a great amount of pressure.

Business executives are not entirely trusted. There are too many tales of CEOs who are undeniably brilliant but resort to the most underhanded tactics to get their staff to fall in line, improve their bottom line, and take out the competition.

Labor union leaders are not particularly anyone's favorite, because again, there is a lot of manipulation and deals that need to be made, and the temptation to cut corners or do something other than was promised remains very high.

Lawyers can often stray easily into being deceptive. Whether it is altruistic—as in wanting to help their innocent clients—or more from a personal need to win, many cases have lawyers crossing lines that they should not to get their wins.

Real estate agents are pretty suspect sometimes, presenting a pretty picture only for the brand-new homeowner to learn many terrible things after purchasing or paying the lease.

This does not imply that everyone in the industries mentioned above is a deceiver or a Machiavellian, or anything like that. It just means that these professions would work well for a liar and most likely would have a significant number of people for whom lying is as natural as breathing.

Politics and Manipulation

Now you will look at tactics that politicians use to get people to vote for them and support their policies even when it actually would not serve anyone besides themselves.

Appealing to their national pride: One of the ways politicians can get people on their side is by appealing to their national pride. A politician's power is dependent on their ability to get the people to willingly accept their legitimacy, authority, and right to get them to pay taxes. Plus, if a politician can continue to get people to back up the government and the country just because they all belong on the same piece of land and recognize a certain flag as theirs, they can continue to grow in power and influence.

The trouble is that it is not rational to selflessly support a group as far as the average voter is concerned. For this reason, the politician will speak about lofty ideals, worthy causes, and higher values. They will speak of "the great red, white and blue" and serving the country. It's not a coincidence that politicians focus on such ephemeral and vague ideals.

While a persuasive tactic would be getting people to see "What's in it for me," this doesn't play out well in politics since what works even better than social exchange is an appeal to identity. Think about it: If the populace were to think long and hard about what is in it for them if they vote someone in or back them up, they would realize the answer to that question is "Nothing."

Sculpting their voters: Another thing politicians do is carefully sculpt their voters. As Robert Cialdini once wrote, "We like people who are like us," and as such, it is important to the politician to seem like they represent the citizens in many ways. In other words, the politician has to seem like the prototype of the people. Think of George Bush, with his Bushisms, errors in speech, seeming disdain for the bigwigs in DC, and love for steak and beer. He came off looking like the average voter, and that was a genius move on his part, whether or not people got any good out of his administration. You could argue that Bush was the perfect Machiavellian in that he presented his weakness as his most representative quality—which automatically meant he could not possibly be attacked for it. Even when enemies would attack this seeming weakness, all it did was make him stronger.

Creating a sense of community: Politicians also know the importance of creating a community, a bunch of "us," with no "I" in existence. This is how they can get the populace to stop thinking about themselves and think more about the government's interests. The goal is to get people to be less selfish and more focused on the "collective"—except the collective is the politician and their ideals.

Throwing the masses a bone: The higher up you rise in politics, the more you risk losing touch with the grassroots. However, it is also true that the higher you rise, the more leverage you will get when you make yourself accessible to the electorate. The reason for this is simple: If you, as powerful as you are, can come down to their level and be accessible, that will make the public look at you as someone who is very magnanimous. In other words, the best politicians know how important it is to throw the masses a bone.

To understand this phenomenon, just know that the voters would rather have a leader just like them and close to them. If a leader seems too detached or too high up like a king, their followers more likely than not will not willingly put themselves on the line for them or their causes. A politician knows the importance of seeming like they are not just in it for the people; they're in it right beside them. Seeming like they're great friends with the average Joe naturally endears them to everyone.

Creating their enemies: The Machiavellian knows not to make enemies. Instead, they create foes. They can use the enemy like a pawn for their internal power struggles. They work with the mindset that the enemy of their enemy is their friend.

They can also get into an untouchable friendship with a much stronger enemy, allowing for oppression to continue endlessly, like how China defends North Korean dictators. A politician also knows that when they have an enemy, they can use them to generate massive support and trample down all opposition.

The reason this works is brilliant and yet simple. As humans, people have evolved to put aside their differences and come together when faced with mutual enemies. This unity is formed with the politician right at the core of everyone's power, of course. This is why you would be hard-pressed to find a good politician who does not have enemies.

Being unfair to the outliers: The politician is not fair. It is what it is. Even great leaders are never fair. Sure, they will be fair to those who support them, but they will definitely not bother with being fair to those who do not, and this is how they continue to strengthen their leadership.

Every politician understands that the constituency they represent will expect some favorable policies. Everyone knows this is often the case. Even referees judge much more leniently when their home team commits the offense. Some politicians will go as far as pandering only to the interests of their ingroups, to the point where others begin to suffer so that they can get more support from those groups.

Embodying the country: The politician who is smart and persuasive will convince voters that they and they alone are the embodiment of the nation and all its values. When a politician presented themselves this way, automatically they move from being just flesh and blood to become an actual mirror image of the nation, one that is "selfless." When people begin putting up pictures of politicians in their home, that is a sure sign that those politicians have succeeded.

For a moment, think back to Ronald Reagan and his administration, where he was presented as the embodiment of all things American. The Assistant White House Chief of Staff at the time, Richard G. Darman, actually wrote this at the start of Ron's campaign: "Paint RR as the personification of all that is right with or heroized by America. Leave Mondale in a position where an attack on Reagan is tantamount to an attack on America's idealized image of itself—where a vote against Reagan is in some subliminal sense, a vote against mythic 'AMERICA.'"

Reagan did wind up becoming the living embodiment of the values of capitalism and freedom, and so did America, and this started a cycle that powered itself by itself. Of course, it also helped that Reagan was a natural enemy of the USSR. As far as the American public was concerned, it was not the president of the USA taking on the president of the USSR. For them, it was the living embodiment of capitalism and freedom taking on the communists. In other words, it was much bigger in the minds of the American public than what it really was, and this further cemented the idea that Reagan was a man of the people, by the people, for the people.

The "Great Leader" scam: When the people call on a politician rather than the politician having to push themselves onto the people, they have the best situation ever. It is awesome for them when the people believe that they and they alone can get the job done, whatever it is. In fact, here is the perfect cocktail to political power: Have an enemy, a war to wage, and be the perfect picture of a resolute, tough leader who will take no guff. It would be hard to keep people from voting for such a leader in droves.

This works because crowds will often go to the leader with the most charisma so that they can submit their will to them. This is especially the case when the country is going through a tough time with crisis after crisis. So, for this reason, the dominant leader will continue to promote models of leadership that are individualistic by saying or implying things like how the country needs strong leaders— like themselves. They will also sway the electorate about the troubles and uncertainties in the land — "Let the people state their choice!"

Pretending to be uninterested in power: If a politician looks like they are not interested in power and are in it for the people, they will get all the support they need. So, the politician will go on and on about how they are committed to making beneficial changes for their constituencies without mentioning their actual motives.

People prefer leaders who ignore the benefits of being leaders than those who are only in it for themselves. The politician knows they have to be proponents of major causes like reforms. They will talk about the need for change or to fight this enemy or another. Inevitably, this garners support from the grassroots.

Now take a look at Roosevelt, the one president who ran for a third mandate, and then a fourth. That said, by the end of his second one, things did not seem so clear. If he were definite about what he intended to do, he would have had to deal with a lot of trouble and been accused of being an autocrat.

Roosevelt said he wanted a third mandate. However, he never flat-out said he did not, either, as that would have made it difficult for him to change his mind. Instead, he worked in the background so that all of the other candidates who mattered would not look particularly strong. Roosevelt was a skilled politician and manipulator. He molded himself into the "great leader" by making it clear there was no other or better candidate who could do the job of leading America. With the ongoing war, he deliberately used outside enemies as leverage. Additionally, he acted like he was only serving out of a sense of duty and not because he wanted power.

This section is not meant to bash politics. It is just saying that this field is very attractive to power-hungry people. It's attractive to people like Machiavellians. In the end, they are all just people, for the most part. Do not misconstrue this as some argument for why people should do away with politics altogether. Without it, societies would probably be worse off.

The point here is to help you see how manipulative, persuasive, and deceptive tactics are used in politics. When you know how the game works, you can take an active, more informed role in the governance of your nation as well. Politics should never be up to politicians alone. Everyone is in this together. Thus, you should know how it all works for gaming the system for the greater good or telling when a politician is hoodwinking the entire nation.

Chapter Eleven: Learning to Spot Deception

Body language matters in life. If you notice that the body language and words of the person you are dealing with do not quite match up, there is trouble. Sure, some clues indicate the possibility that someone's telling an outright lie, or they are keeping the truth hidden from you.

When it comes to communication, a lot goes on beyond just speaking, listening, and understanding. Some lies are told only as a matter of courtesy. Say someone asks you how you are. You probably would not want to dump on them about how your lover left you, and your left hip hurts terribly for some reason. You wouldn't get in trouble for telling these lies. Just realize that these are lies that people tend to tell every day.

Lying is incredibly common and sometimes expected. There are even legal strategies that allow for "plausible deniability." So, it is helpful to know how to spot deception so that when you're in a situation where anything less than the truth wouldn't do, you can make sure to get to the bottom of the matter.

The Right and Wrong Ways to Spot Deception

Focusing on eye movement or body language alone is not enough. Many studies have shown that trying to read a lie using body language or eye movement is not effective—even for professional interrogators and law enforcement.

The research on deception has been disappointing for the most part. A lot of it involved trying to gauge the liar's intent by looking at their body language or facial expressions like darting eyes, blushing cheeks, and nervous laughter. Think back to Bill Clinton when he touched his nose as he claimed not to have had an affair with Monica Lewinsky. Everyone assumed that meant he was lying. The thing about lying is that it often generates really intense feelings of guilt, nerves, and sometimes excitement at the prospect of getting away with it. These emotions are difficult to keep in check, so even when you think you have a poker face on, you still have a few "tells" that give you away. These tells are called micro expressions.

The trouble is that the more psychologists dive into the matter, the more they find it difficult to grasp any clues that are reliable enough to let you know when someone is lying. The thing about human behavior is that there is so much variety to it. With enough time, and after becoming very familiar with someone, you might be able to tell what their tics are when they are honest versus when they're shady. However, you cannot apply what you learn about how they act in both situations to other people, as it differs from person to person. In other words, body language has no dictionary that you can reliably turn to when you're confused about what someone's body is saying. There are no signs that always come up when it comes to deception. For some folks, they giggle when they lie. Others get much more serious. Some make heavy eye contact, and some avoid it altogether. There is just no cue you can turn to and say, "Aha! There's the sign that they're lying to me." Even the theory that the subconscious mind can tell when someone is lying or picking up on these cues has been proven untrue.

Despite this, you must still learn when you're being had, and it almost seems like all you have are these cues, almost as mythical as a unicorn. So, you need a way to figure out how to find out when you're being deceived. What do you do? Focus on the liar's words. It's better to ignore all of the subtle cues and mannerisms that people give off when they're lying and instead focus on gently teasing the truth out of them by asking questions until their story starts to crumble. Here is what you need to do:

1. *Make use of open questions.* When you ask open questions, this forces the deceiver to expand their story until they are completely trapped in their lies.

2. *Use the element of surprise to your advantage.* If you want to know if someone is lying, you have to give them much more work. This means asking them questions they do not expect or that are a bit confusing. You can also ask for their version of events, but backward.

3. *Look out for small details that you can verify.* Say someone tells you they study at Harvard—ask them what it is like going there each day. If you notice they said something that is not true, don't let on that you are on to them. Allow them to grow in confidence, and watch as they prattle on with more lies.

4. *Notice how their confidence changes.* Pay attention to the liar and see how their manner of speech changes whenever you decide to challenge them. They might be really talkative when they feel like they are the one in control of the conversation, but if they feel they're losing control, they might decide to clam up and say no more or speak in monotones.

You want to have a casual conversation with them. Do not go "all interrogator" on them. Keep the pressure gentle, and this will be more than enough for the lair to eventually slip up and show their hand by either saying something that doesn't align with the story they have said so far or by getting evasive or responding erratically. Recall that there is no such thing as a magic bullet when it comes to catching liars. It's about taking all the things that actually work and using them to get results.

Information Trumps a Confession

This is something that is always used in Britain. On account of a ton of false confessions during the mid-80s, the British courts made it official that law enforcement was no longer allowed to use force or aggression to get information out of their suspects. The interrogations are also taped to make sure the officers comply with the new interrogation method, which involves having a chat with the prisoner and beginning with asking questions that the interrogator already knows the answer to. This has helped to reduce the number of false confessions dramatically.

Cheryl Hiscock-Anisman,a forensic psychologist, working at the National University in La Jolla, California, and Kevin Colwell, a forensic scientist, working in Southern Connecticut State University, New Haven, have spent years researching interrogation. They have both realized that those who cook up a story would often cook up an easy to recall script that would be difficult to poke holes in. Those who are honest don't have to use a script since it really did happen as they say it did, and they were there. So, the honest ones will make mistakes, and not only that, they will bring in detail that is unrelated to support their case.

Both Hiscock-Anisman and Colwell have been hard at work to make the contrast between deceivers and honest people much more obvious. Taking what they have learned into the field, they've spent time training officers to look out for patterns in speech misteach of body language and cues. While the San Diego Police Department was, at first, skeptical about their methods, they've since added this method to their toolbox of interrogation methods.

Another thing that helps decide who is lying is to ask the simplest questions. So, the interviewer only has to focus on the words and verbal cues of the person speaking and not the nonverbal stuff. The researchers say it's best to start with a nonthreatening question. For instance, you can ask them what their day was like. They are not likely to lie to you about that—unless they just murdered someone that day and hid the body. The answer will also involve a vivid memory. Coupled with an honest answer, that should give you a baseline for what they are like when they're honest. You know how much information and detail they typically provide when talking about true things.

After establishing a baseline of honesty with the person being interviewed, you can then ask them to let you know about the actual issue at hand or being investigated. When they are done recounting the events, you have to take a step back and compare their responses to both stories. Have you noticed that they use the same number of descriptive phrases? Was there any recall, and was it the same as the first time around? Keep these things in mind as they help you know whether or not you are being lied to.

After this, you must ask a harder question, one which will often give away who is lying and who's being honest. You can say, "Okay, can you go back to when this all happened and walk me through everything again, but do it backward, okay?" What happens all the time is that the liar will have a lot of trouble answering that one. This is a nifty little trick to have for the next time your teenager lies about what they were doing out so late.

Science has shown that when someone is telling the truth, they will give you many little facts. They will give you anecdotal details because they lived the situation as they say they did. In fact, honest people have been proven to give thirty percent more detail than liars.

Truths About Lies

First of all, the perfect liar does not exist. While lying happens every day, it is not something that comes naturally to most people. Often there will be some emotional tell or something that can and will give them away. Another thing is that most people suck at figuring out deception. In other words, as terrible as most people are at lying, they are just as bad at detecting lies.

Now, you cannot go off of blinking alone, but lying can affect how much a liar blinks. A 2008 research article by Stephen Porter and Leanne Brinke of the Forensic Psychology lab at Dalhousie University showed that people who kept their emotions hidden would blink at a much different rate. If they were masking their emotions, they would blink faster. If they were neutralizing the emotions, they would blink a lot slower.

You should also know that it is much harder to fake negative feelings than positive ones. This same article from 2008 showed that it's harder to act sad, fearful, or disgusted than to act happy. According to University of Buffalo's Dr. Mark Frank in a 2013 **PopSci article**, it's harder to fake negative emotions because when you're not feeling great, while one part of the brain works to make you feel how you feel, another works to keep the expression in check. Typically, you wouldn't have this tug of war going on when you're feeling happy.

Liars will often use many different words than those who tell the truth. In that 2012 study, it was demonstrated that they would use many more tentative words and speak a lot less.

An interesting thing about lies is that it is hard to lie to someone if you are attracted to them. Another study carried out in 1985 by DePaulo, Stone, and Lassiter, titled *Telling Ingratiating Lies: Effects of Target Sex and Target Attractiveness on verbal and nonverbal deceptive success,* focused on white lies that people tell to make sure everyone gets along. In this study, all the participants had to act like they agreed with other people on subjects they really did not agree on. They were also asked to act as if they disagreed with them on matters that actually agreed on.

The scientists referred to these two deceptions as:

    1. Ingratiating lies

    2. Non-ingratiating lies, respectively

The researchers also had the subjects tell both uningratiating truths and ingratiating truths throughout the study. In the end, it was easier to see the ingratiating lies more than the non-ingratiating ones. The lies were even easier to spot when it was the opposite sex listening to them. Additionally, the more attractive the subject being lied to was, the easier it was to catch on to the lies.

What is funny is the way the lies were spotted. The ingratiating lies were easy to figure out using visual cues such as facial expressions. Meanwhile, lies to the less interesting subject were easier to deduce using auditory cues like vocal tone.

The Mouth versus The Eyes

Many people, when they are faking their feelings, will often let it slip through their eyes. Remember the micro expressions detailed earlier? It is hard to pick up on these, especially because the mouth works hard and effectively at keeping eye movements hidden.

When people are pretending to feel things, the micro expressions will pop up and show their honest feelings, and then right after those micro expressions, the mouth will smile or do something else to hide the real truth of their emotions. The mouth is so effective at hiding the truth that it will often be more than enough to help the eyes escape detection even when the interrogator is focused on the eyes alone. It is simple: People cannot look at eyes without looking at the mouth, and vice versa. Another note to keep in mind: Timing is important. If the smile happens first, it's not masking the eyes. If it comes right after the eyes give off their micro expression, it is masking it. This is why it's not all that easy to figure out lies using just body language and facial expression alone, even when the liar isn't great at lying.

When you cheat, it is easy to forget the morals you hold dear so that you do not have to deal with uncomfortable feelings of cognitive dissonance. In a study titled *Dishonest Deed, Clear Conscience: When Cheating Leads to Moral Disengagement and Motivated*

Forgetting, by Shu, Gono, and Bazerman, published in the Personality and Social Psychology Bulletin in 2011, the researchers found that when we cheat or are dishonest, we disengage from our morals and are motivated to forget about whatever concepts of right and wrong we hold dear.

The study showed that the ones who went on to cheat had selectively less memory retention for information that would be deemed morally relevant. Another thing to note is that their memories were no different from those who chose not to cheat before the task began. The difference in memories showed up after. So, cheating made them forget the rules.

Finally, saying to people, "Don't be a liar" works much better than telling them, "Don't lie." Sure, some people get a kick out of cheating, but most people want to do right at the end of the day. Research shows that while people might not mind lying or cheating, no one wants to be labeled a liar or cheater. So, the next time you are dealing with a liar, you can try the "Don't be a liar" statement on them and see if that encourages them to take a few leaps closer to the truth.

Chapter Twelve: Becoming Less Vulnerable

This book wraps up with ways to keep yourself safe and free from the machinations of the Machiavellian. You will learn how to remain impermeable to their antics and be less vulnerable than the average person.

Dealing with Negotiations

How do you deal when you are attacked during a negotiation? Whether you want to call it emotional intelligence or reverse psychology, what you're going to learn right now is something called tactical empathy. This is the weapon you will use to stave off the Machiavellian's attacks. It is anything but the norm. It's very counter-intuitive, but it works. You just need to have the grit to see it through.

First, note the opposite of what the negotiator is upset about. So, what you need to do is simply say, "It seems like you like to . . ." and then end the sentence with the opposite of whatever it is they are whining about. You should be prepared for the spectacle of watching a speeding train come to a complete stop on account of loads of confusion coursing through their mind. How exactly do you pull this off, and what is the reason it works?

The thing is that for every like, there is an equal disciple. If there is something they are coming at you for, you want to go at them for a contrast they value. When you label what they're doing or saying, you're basically triggering their amygdala so that it releases some feel-good dopamine and serotonin. Consider this: If you are dealing with a landlord who does not allow people to sublet their apartments, it means they value stability more than anything. If you're dealing with a landlord who is not open to renegotiations, they obviously think stability is a virtue.

Many objections that come up in the process of negotiation are often founded on uncertainty. You should be the one person keeping a cool head by courageously calling it as you see it. Label the precise fear that they are dealing with. If you really want to get into it, you might want to label it the inverse positive.

Say your neighborhood Mach is attacking something that you really care about or a hot-button issue. Assume that you love to work out, and they say something like, "Working out is incredibly stupid and vain. You're just trying to show you're fitter than I am by doing this workout program." What do you say in response? You could say, "It sounds like you like being with folks who you feel are your equals."

You want to follow up on these labels with a pause. Be silent after that. Allow it to really sink into their noggin and work its way through their body. Do not break the silence first.

You may feel like you don't have the quick wit to label something at the moment, but you do. You only need to practice, and then you will do this naturally. So, just say the words, "It sounds like you like . . ." and wrap up the sentence. Whatever you do, do not turn away from them. Don't speak. Wait. The more you practice doing this, the better you will get at it. Just doing this five times a day for three to four days straight should yield remarkable results. Whenever you're negotiating, keep in mind that you always want to do the counter-intuitive things. This is how you get the upper hand. This labeling technique will land you much better deals than you thought you could get.

The Number One Vulnerability: Thinking You're Too Smart

You might think that you are way too smart to be had by the Machiavellian and other deceptive personalities, but chances are you aren't—and this isn't an insult. You must get rid of that notion because it is exactly what makes you vulnerable to deception. In a book titled *The Confidence Game*, written by Maria Konnikova, there is a lot of information on why people fall for con men and their scams. The con man's victim is not just ignorant and foolish; they're also regular folks who are desperate at that moment or too emotional to see what's really going on.

Most leaders are proud of the fact that they are strategic and logical. Yet Konikova warns that pride is the beginning of the end. Pride blinds you to the Machiavellian's wiles.

The funny thing about past American presidents is that the best ones are humble, while the worst are ineffective and prideful. They were rarely ever open to admitting they were wrong about something, and it was even harder still to own up to their mistakes because they'd had way too much experience—enough to make them think they were above being fallible. However, the great presidents were open, humble, and honest about their weaknesses.

Following this logic, here is a fact that will surprise you: The only other person who can be conned besides the prideful, emotional, or ignorant is the con man himself—as he feels untouchable, immune to ever being stupid enough to fall for a scheme like his. The more you assume you are aware, the easier it is for you to get deeper and deeper into self-deception, which leaves you open to being deceived by other people around you.

Self-Deceit, Denial, and Immunity

There was once a con artist named Fred Demara. He was one of the best the world had ever seen. He had impersonated everyone from businessmen to doctors to priests. During the Korean war, he pretended to be a trauma surgeon aboard a Canadian destroyer. He was able to carry out surgeries just using a manual an actual doctor had written for him.

This same Frank had commissioned a writer to do a biography on him, only to steal the writer's identity. As if things could not get bizarre enough, the biographer whose identity was stolen spent many years later defending him! The people Frank had played for a fool would go the extra mile for him, time after time. The reason for this is that they were not willing to accept that they'd been had—and Frank was well aware of this tendency and exploited it.

Think about this for a minute. Studies by Harvard University and Startup Compass show that not wanting to let a business plan go makes it much less likely that a company will go public. There are too many CEOs and business leaders who do wrong by their employees and their organizations by placing more importance on the appearance of a strong, bulldog leadership, rather than being willing and flexible to go back on their decision or employ a different strategy that can help take their business to groundbreaking heights. The leaders who wind up being fooled are the ones who first fool themselves.

How Not to Be an Idiot

Pride is part of being human. The downside to pride is that it is often lauded as an admirable thing, like taking pride in your work, your abilities, and so on. This is inevitably what opens you up to being deceived—first by yourself and then by others. So, the questions become: How can you avoid this happening? Or how can you not be an idiot?

You must be okay with admitting that you are/might be wrong. In his autobiography, Benjamin Franklin wrote about his decision to start being forthright when he felt he could be wrong as he made his arguments. He noted that since choosing to do this and listening to people he disagreed with rather than waiting to re-emphasize his perception or point of view, he had slashed down his fear of not being right. Here are the man's words so that you can learn from them:

"I made it a rule to forbear all direct contradictions to the sentiments of others and all positive assertion of my own. I even forbade myself the use of every word or expression in the language that imported a fixed opinion, such as 'certainly,' 'undoubtedly,' etc. I adopted instead of them 'I conceive,' 'I apprehend,' or 'I imagine' a thing to be so and so; or 'so it appears to me at present.'

"When another asserted something that I thought an error, I denied myself the pleasure of contradicting him abruptly, and of showing him immediately some absurdity in his proposition. In answering, I began by observing that in certain cases or circumstances, his opinion would be right, but in the present case, there appeared or seemed to be some difference, etc. I soon found the advantage of this change in my approach. The conversations I engaged in went on more pleasantly. The modest way in which I proposed my opinions procured them a readier reception and less contradiction. I had less mortification when I was found to be in the wrong, and I more easily prevailed with others to give up their mistakes and join with me when I happened to be in the right."

You can read Benjamin Franklin's autobiography to learn more about the strategy, which helped the man be much less prideful—or less of an idiot. So, whatever you do, always be open to changing your mind about people, situations, or strategies. Be flexible, and it will be easier for you to notice when you are about to be had. If you're so desperate to have and keep a good reputation, you're going to be a prime target for a Machiavellian. Plus, even after they have had their way with you, you're still going to be self-deluded, refusing to acknowledge you've been taken for a ride. Do not be that person. Don't be an idiot.

Conclusion

You have finally arrived at the end of this book, and the odds are that you have learned a lot about lies, liars, Machiavellians, and their scheming. Never again do you have to allow yourself to become a victim of this set of unscrupulous people.

One other thing to point out is that it is not enough to read one book and assume you do not need to continue to learn about the process of deception. The reason you should continue to educate yourself is simple: Every day, especially with technology and all sorts of innovations coming up, deception is becoming easier and easier to get away with, especially when it comes to the media and political power.

You should go through this book again and mark up sections that stand out. Practice what you have learned so that you become more confident in facing down people who deceive you, or even better, waiting for an opportune time to turn the tables on them and show them to the world for what they really are.

You have done a very smart thing buying this book, and you are even better off for having read it. You do not have to be like the rest of the world—gullible to devious people. You, for once, can take back control of your life. It must be reiterated that the information you have learned within the pages of this book is incredibly potent, and you have to use it responsibly, and preferably, for good.

Never assume for one minute that you are too brilliant to be scammed or deceived. Even the most brilliant minds have been had. You do not have to fall prey to that anymore. If you learn nothing else from this book, keep in mind that you should always be honest and above board in all you do because it serves you better in the long run. At times in this book, the thought might have occurred to you that it would probably serve you to emulate the Machiavellian. The truth is, yes, it will, but only for the short run, and after that, you will have a very difficult time getting people to trust you. You don't want this. So, in everything you do, be honest, open, humble, and remember: Anyone can be a victim. You will not ever be a victim again if you consider that you're not above being deceived.

Here's another book by Neil Morton that you might like

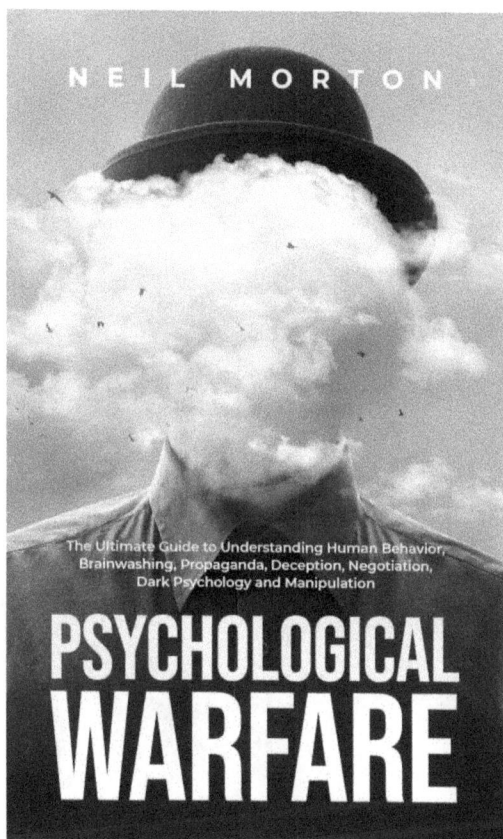

NEIL MORTON

The Ultimate Guide to Understanding Human Behavior, Brainwashing, Propaganda, Deception, Negotiation, Dark Psychology and Manipulation

PSYCHOLOGICAL WARFARE

www.ingramcontent.com/pod-product-compliance
Lightning Source LLC
Chambersburg PA
CBHW070759300326
41914CB00053B/738